# MARCO ⊕ POLO

D1287931

# COR FU

SERBIA
MNE RKS
BUL.
MAC. (F.Y.R.O.M)
Bari  ALBANIA
ITALY
TURKEY
Corfu  Igoumenitsa
Athens
Sicily
(I)
MALTA  GREECE
Crete
*Mediterranean Sea*
LIBYA

# EDGARTOWN

## Free Public Library

THE GREATEST OF ALL our American institutions is our system of public libraries. No
country has anything like it. If you've tried to
do research or work with libraries overseas and
abroad you are immediately reminded how fortu-
nate we are. We just take it for granted.
— David McCullough

Presented by

26 West Tisbury Road
Edgartown, Mass. 02539

shows you the way...

including routes and offline maps!

# GET MORE OUT OF YOUR MARCO POLO GUIDE

IT'S AS SIMPLE AS THIS

**1** go.marco-polo.com/cor

**2** download and discover

# GO!

WORKS OFFLINE!

**6  INSIDER TIPS**
Our top 15 Insider Tips

**8  BEST OF...**
- ● Great places for free
- ● Only on Corfu
- ● And if it rains?
- ● Relax and chill out

**12  INTRODUCTION**
Discover Corfu!

**18  WHAT'S HOT**
There are lots of new things to
discover on Corfu

**20  IN A NUTSHELL**
Background information on
Corfu

**26  FOOD & DRINK**
Top culinary tips

**30  SHOPPING**
For a fun-filled shopping spree!

**32  CORFU TOWN**

**48  THE NORTH**
48 Acharávi & Róda   56 Ágios
Geórgios & Co.  58 Kassiópi
63 Paleokastrítsa

**68  THE SOUTH**
68 Ágios Geórgios South
73 Ágios Górdis   75 Messongí-
Moraítika

**80  CENTRAL CORFU**
81 Dafníla & Dassiá   86 Guviá
& Kontokáli   88 Pélekas, Glifáda & Mirtiótissa

**SYMBOLS**

| | |
|---|---|
| INSIDER TIP | Insider Tip |
| ★ | Highlight |
| ●●●● | Best of... |
| � | Scenic view |
| ♺ | Responsible travel: for eco-logical or fair trade aspects |
| (*) | Telephone numbers that are not toll-free |

**PRICE CATEGORIES HOTELS**

| | |
|---|---|
| *Expensive* | over 100 euros |
| *Moderate* | 60–100 euros |
| *Budget* | under 60 euros |

Prices for a double room,
without breakfast, in the high
season

**PRICE CATEGORIES RESTAURANTS**

| | |
|---|---|
| *Expensive* | over 20 euros |
| *Moderate* | 15–20 euros |
| *Budget* | under 15 euros |

Prices for a meat dish with
potatoes, a Greek salad and
half a bottle of house wine

# CONTENTS

94 **DISCOVERY TOURS**
94 Corfu at a glance  99 Ancient Kérkyra – a walking tour outside the old town  102 Villages and beaches around the

Pantokrátor  105 Shopping in Corfu style between Guviá and Paleokastrítsa  107 Boat trip to Albania

110 **SPORTS & ACTIVITIES**
Activities for all seasons

114 **TRAVEL WITH KIDS**
Best things to do with kids

118 **FESTIVALS & EVENTS**
All dates at a glance

120 **LINKS, BLOGS, APPS & MORE**
Plan ahead and use on the go

122 **TRAVEL TIPS**
From A to Z

128 **USEFUL PHRASES**

132 **ROAD ATLAS**

142 **INDEX & CREDITS**

144 **DOS & DON'TS**

**DID YOU KNOW?**
Timeline → p. 14
Family and other animals → p. 24
Local specialities → p. 28
The fish cult→ p. 75
Esoteric centres→ p. 78
Versatile little oranges → p. 92
National holidays → p. 119
Budgeting → p. 123
For bookworms and film buffs→ p. 124
Currency converter → p. 126
Weather → p. 127

**MAPS IN THE GUIDEBOOK**
(134 A1) Page numbers and coordinates refer to the road atlas
(0) Site/address located off the map. Coordinates are also given for places that are not marked on the road atlas
(U A1) refers to the map of Corfu Town (Kérkyra) inside the back cover

(*Ⅲ A1*) refers to the removable pull-out map
(*Ⅲ a1*) refers to the inset map on the pull-out map

**INSIDE FRONT COVER:**
The best highlights

**INSIDE BACK COVER:**
Map of Corfu Town (Kérkyra)

# The best MARCO POLO Insider Tips

## Our top 15 Insider Tips

**INSIDER TIP** **Order differently**

At the *Ektós Skédio,* the waiter lets you do part of the work. You fill in an order form – and he brings lots of Corfiot delicacies → **p. 43**

**INSIDER TIP** **Alternative nights**

Corfu's alternatie scene parties the night away at the *Polytéchno.* Their motto: experiments instead of mainstream. They also have stand-up comedy and animated movies → **p. 46**

**INSIDER TIP** **Royal bay**

Only a few visitors to Corfu know about the small bay in *Mon Repos* Park where royalty used to bathe → **p. 101**

**INSIDER TIP** **Relax in a lemon grove**

The *Lemon Garden* in Acharávi is the place to sit – central, but completely secluded – and enjoy a drink, cake or fine food surrounded by citrus trees. The taverna even hosts Alexis Zorba once a week → **p. 50**

**INSIDER TIP** **Alternative accomodation**

The *Pélekas Country Club* offers stylish residence on a Venetian estate secluded away from the crowds and traffic noise → **p. 91**

**INSIDER TIP** **Lobster without frills**

The *Gregóris* taverna is located off the beaten track above the usually deserted Astrakéri Beach and serves lobsters at reasonable prices, prepared just the way the fishermen themselves like them → **p. 53**

**INSIDER TIP** **Greek alarm clock**

If you go to sleep in the traditional no-frills hotel *Konstantinoúpolis* on the Old Port, you'll be awakened at eight o'clock sharp by the Greek national anthem → **p. 46**

**INSIDER TIP** **An evening by the sea**

Coastal cliffs, palm trees, the sea and wooden jettys have never looked more atmospheric than from the bar *La Grotta* in Paleokastrítsa → **p. 65**

INSIDER TIP **Keep fit**
The *Corfu Mountainbike Shop* in Dassiá offers everything a biker needs. The services offered by the MTB pros range from rentals to guided day tours and a complete Fly-&-Bike programme → p. 112

INSIDER TIP **A family paradise**
Children and their parents can spend carefree days in the apartments in the *Honey Valley,* where the little ones can find lots of things to do → p. 58

INSIDER TIP **Now this is a beach hotel**
No other hotel on the island is closer to the beach than the *Dassiá Beach.* Only the shady taverna fits between the lobby and the beach → p. 84

INSIDER TIP **In an enchanted forest**
Drive slowly, then get out of the car! And take in the ancient *olive forest* between Pentáti and Paramónas with its rays of sun, nylon nets, chicken and sheep → p. 98

INSIDER TIP **Riding for everyone**
Sally-Ann Lewis used to be a cowgirl in Wyoming. Since 1992, she has been taking riders of all levels on two-hour trails through Corfu's olive groves and vineyards. *Trailriders'* stables are near the village of Áno Korakiána → p. 112

INSIDER TIP **Pink flamingos**
In the salines of *Alikés,* hundreds of pink flamingos standing on one leg can often be seen in the months between October and May. The vast birds' sanctuary is only accessible via narrow paths, and its edge, you can even bathe all on your own → p. 73

INSIDER TIP **Hike across the island**
You can hike across the island on the 220 km (136 miles) long *Corfu Trail* (photo below). You should be something of a trailblazer; the paths are not perfectly marked but there is always a village in sight on Corfu → p. 112

# BEST OF...

**FOR FREE**

● *Free culture*
Rock festivals, jazz concerts, operas and concerts with traditional Corfiot orchestras – and all free of charge or for a token 1 cent fee! On no less than 30 evenings between early June and mid August the annual *International Festival of Corfu* bans boredom from the island → p. 119

● *Panorama with airplanes*
The panoramic view from the free *Kanóni* lookout point near the town towards Mouse Island and the monastery island of Vlachérna in the foreground is magnificent (photo). Fun can be had watching the jets full of holidaymakers swooping down at eye-level and guessing where they will land on the runway → p. 38, 116

● *Corfu's island brewery*
The *Corfu Brewery* near Arillás offers free admission to its small private brewery offering visitors the chance not only to try the beer but also to see how it is made. Six different beers are produced on site and visitors can taste all of them → p. 56

● *From pool to pool*
How about a bit of pool-hopping? You can often *swim in the pools* at many smaller hotels even if you are not a guest – as long as you buy a drink at the bar. A change of scenery is always good → p. 72

● *Open invitation to night-owls*
Nightlife in Corfu Town is not nearly as expensive as you might think. Very few of the venues in the popular clubbing district around the ferry terminal charge entry fees. Get ready to party the night away → p. 45

● *A table with a view – and a sunbed*
If you choose to have lunch in the beautifully situated *Panórama* taverna in Petríti you can indulge in a further luxury free of charge after an excellent meal – namely the use of sunbeds on the beach nearby → p. 79

◖◗◖◗ Dots in guidebook refer to "Best of..." tips

● *Watch out – keep your head down!*
The Corfiots celebrate *Easter* in their own very special way. On Easter Saturday hundreds of clay water jugs are thrown out of windows and from balconies onto the streets in the Old Town. Thousands of cheerful spectators watch this wet spectacle that follows the magnificent Easter procession → p. 118

● *Little oranges are big business*
The bitter fruit of the *cumquat tree* has become a new trademark of the island. Try them yourself! Liqueurs, jams, sweets and many other goodies can be found in the shop run by the *Vassilákis family* in the town or its sales rooms at Achíllion (photo) → p. 44, 92

● *A lifetime working with olive wood*
Olive trees provide fruit and oil as well as a unique kind of wood that demands great skill from carvers. For decades Thomás has been one of the best and has devoted himself to this craft in his studio *By Tom* in Corfu's Old Town → p. 44

● *Moments of contemplation*
Linger for a while in Corfu's most important church *Ágios Spirídonas* and experience the locals' religious tradition first hand. There is a continuous stream of Corfiots who kiss the icons, pay homage to the relics of the patron saint of the island and kneel in prayer, as many feel this is the place – between paintings, icons and the silver sarcophagus of St Spirídon – where heaven and earth meet → p. 34

● *Fish in the Garden of Eden*
Corfiots love lush gardens and a fish soup called *bourdétto* made with scorpion fish. In *Alonáki* Taverna near Chalikúnas you can enjoy the best of both – a version of the traditional dish made to a particularly tasty recipe, served in beautiful surroundings → p. 70

● *In perfect harmony*
Dance like Zorba the Greek! Thanks to the blockbuster film of the same name, the *sirtáki* has become synonymous with Greek dancing. You can delight in watching professional dancers perform on the terrace at the *Golden Beach* bar and actually give it a try yourself! → p. 77

# BEST OF...

● **Snails and mussels**
Amateur biologists, divers and sea life enthusiasts will be fascinated by the amazing deep seabed discoveries on exhibition at the *Shell Museum* in Benítses → p. 77

● **Shopping under the arcades**
The *arcades of the main shopping streets* in the Old Town, especially Odós N. Theotóki, protect shoppers from the scorching heat and downpours → p. 43

● **Jewellery with a personal touch**
Shells that you find while walking along a beach can be transformed into lovely pieces of jewellery. Corfu's natural jewels can be cast in gold, silver or bronze at *Ílios Living Art* in Ágios Geórgios Pagón → p. 57

● **Just go under**
If you really want to get the better of the rain, just go under water. *Korfu Diving* offers scuba diving and snorkelling for rainy days (photo) → p. 111

● **Journey back in time**
at the *Casa Parlante.* A group of friendly, young people takes you on a tour of this noble mansion once inhabited by a family 200 years ago. Today, this family has been recreated with animated wax figures, which introduce themselves, talk to you, offer a glass of liqueur and even serenade you. You can even take a look around the servant quarters at the end of the tour → p. 38

● **Kama sutra on Corfu**
The ancient Indians were a sensual folk; they engraved the Kama Sutra, or their "verses of desire", into stone and decorated temples with these erotic images. Three examples have made their way inside the *Old Palace* in Corfu Town → p. 40

RAIN

# RELAX AND CHILL OUT
## Take it easy and spoil yourself

● *The perfect treatment*

The *Saint George's Bay Country Club* features a spa in palm tree gardens, a heated 8x25m seawater pool and hammam all surrounded by a splendid hotel which began promoting green living standards long before eco hotels became in vogue → **p. 52**

● *A spot of cricket*

Stop by for a few overs and spend a relaxing Sunday afternoon in the *Café on the Esplanade* in Kérkyra while watching the locals bat and bowl on the well-kept pitch – just like being at home → **p. 37**

● *Secluded beaches*

Have you ever dreamt of having a beach all to yourself? Then hire a motor boat in *Paleokastrítsa* and sail out to one of the bay's many beaches (photo). You will be certain to find one without a bath towel spread out → **p. 65**

● *Romantic ancient temple*

The Romantic painters would surely have set up their easels in front of the tiny *Doric Temple* in the Mon Repos Castle Park. Tourists can also enjoy this romantic setting sitting on the grass between the ancient castle walls – the castle attendants will not escort you off the grass! → **p. 39**

● *Zen as a way of life*

You'll feel like you are in a Buddhist Zen monastery in many meditation houses. Often, day guests are also welcome to come and meditate in Zen-Do and its garden → **p. 78**

● *Awash with orchids*

The romantically inclined will love the *British Cemetery*. In spring and autumn, this fairytale oasis is a mass of wild orchids flowering among the gravestones → **p. 36**

# INTRODUCTION

# DISCOVER CORFU!

Fasten your seat belts, please! Leaving the coast of Italy behind you, your pilot will start his descent where the Adriatic merges into the Ionian Sea. You will be greeted by the first Greek island outcrops before Corfu comes into sight. Even from a height of 4000m, Corfu's beaches are clearly visible; narrow strips of sand hug the many coves along the rugged coastline while wide open bays are fringed with broad sandy beaches in front of green landscape. Your plane descends lower, brushing over a sea of olive trees interspersed with prickly cypresses. Scattered among the hills are dreamy villages dating back centuries. That's where I want to be! On your left, a sea of red roof tiles, two mighty forts and cruise ships docking at the port mark the island's capital on your left. How beautiful it must be!

The plane turns on reaching the radio beacon at Lefkími in the island's south to start its final descent. Green hills shoot by on your left while on your right crowds of people are waving from "mouse island". At this point you might feel a rush of adrenaline or break out into a nervous sweat as it appears the plane is about to nose-dive into the sea. Don't worry though: the cockpit crew expertly land it on the runway that was built in a lagoon. Congratulations, you've arrived on Corfu to start your adventure.

Photo: Kalamáki Beach

It's time to explore *Greece's sixth largest island.* The island's 112,000 inhabitants are also waiting to greet and get to know you. The Corfiots are prepared for foreign guests and well-versed in languages, with most of them speaking *English as well as German and Italian.* This is mainly attributed to the island's history: under Venetian rule for over 400 years, Corfu was then conquered by Napoleon and the French followed by the British. Unification with Greece was only concluded in 1864 after Greece had become independent from the Turks. Corfu was never under Turkish rule however and the island has absorbed far less oriental influence than other Greek islands and mainland regions.

Your first port of call should be Corfu Town. Affordable bus services run between all the main beach resorts and the capital. Known to the Greeks as Kérkyra, Corfu Town is a vibrant place stretching several kilometres directly along the coast. *Sailing yachts, fishing boats, ferries and cruise ships* sail past almost within reach. Land is visible in every direction, from the island's highest mountain (over 900 m/2953 ft ft) in the north to the mountain massifs in North West Greece and Albania on the mainland which are usually covered in snow between November and April. The view alone would be reason enough to visit in winter when the Corfiots are mainly left to their own devices.

> **It is worth visiting the island's capital more than once**

It is worth visiting the island's capital more than once. *Excursion boats* offer trips to Corfu Town from many resorts along the east coast. In the morning you can go

**734 BC**
With the founding of a colony by the Greek city of Corinth, Corfu becomes part of classical Greece

**229 BC**
Corfu is the first Greek town to submit to the rule of the up-and-coming world power Rome

**395–1204 AD**
East-Roman Byzantine period; Corfu ruled from Constantinople

**1386**
The Venetians take over Corfu that develops into one of its most important possessions in the Mediterranean and resists two Turkish conquest campaigns in the 16th century

Empress "Sisi" built it as a holiday home, Kaiser Wilhelm II loved it: Villa Achíllion

shopping – no department stores for a change, but *hundreds of small shops along crooked Old Town lanes* and under shady arcades, where the owners themselves stand behind the counter. On the weekly market, you'll see fish you only know from the aquarium. Watch the hustle and bustle while you enjoy an espresso or a *freddo cappuccino*. After lunch you could chill out *at the Beach Club*, right next to an old Venetian fort.

The Corfiots are among those who observe a siesta in the afternoon, which the Greeks call *ksekúrassi*. This is why there aren't many locals around on streets and squares between 4 and 6pm. After that, the *vólta* begins: the street cafés are crowded, "to see and be seen" is the motto, also for the *4000 students of the island's university*. From 9pm, it's dinnertime – and after midnight, *clubs and discos on the seaside road near the New Port* start to fill up. Dance the night away here better than in any resort. You can always sleep on the beach the next day!

**1453**
The Byzantine Empire collapses; the Turks control all of Greece – with the exception of the Ionian Islands

**1797–1864**
Napoleon occupies the Ionian Islands that subsequently gain independence under Russian and Turkish protection. In 1807, French again; 1809, British; and, after 1815, an independent republic under the protection of Great Britain

**1864**
The Ionian Islands become part of free Greece

**1941–1944**
Italian and German occupation

The island is surrounded by beaches and there is such a great variety that everybody can find that *perfect dream beach*. Those on the east coast facing the mainland, where most of the large seaside hotels are located, are mostly of shingles or smooth pebbles, often several hundred metres long but always fairly narrow. Many of the hotels directly on the beach offset this by providing *lush, green lawns around the pool,* tavernas place deckchairs in their flowery gardens and hang hammocks between the trees. Wooden jetties jut out into the protected bays of the straits. This is where the sun worshippers lie, before climbing down ladders into the water. Some are used as water-sport centres. The east coast is *perfect for waterskiing, paragliding and for paddle boats* – however, surfers will be rather disappointed. This area, with its gently sloping beaches, is ideal for families with children. The bathing shoes that can be bought in any supermarket increase the pleasure even more, and they also protect against the prickly sea urchins.

The north coast is better suited for those who like long, wide beaches. The tavernas and lounge bars make a stopover on *long strolls along the beach* even more enjoyable. It is especially worth visiting them at sunset when the fiery ball sinks into the sea somewhere between the last Greek island of Othoní and the Albanian mainland.

## The west coast has a great variety of beaches

Corfu's west coast facing the open sea offers the *greatest variety of beaches.* They begin at Cape Drástis in the far northwest where the brave climb into the water from *white rocks* and, if the sea is completely calm, swim out along the white sandstone cliffs. Near Peruládes, steps lead down from the steep coast to the long, narrow sandy beach stretching under the cliffs. The golden crescents of sand in the bays of Ágios Stéfanos and Ágios Geórgios Pagón are miles long while most of the 20+ beaches on the fragmented Paleokastritsa Bay are hidden away and *can only be reached by boat.*

*Some large hotels* have opened on the few beaches in the middle of the west coast: in Glifáda, Pélekas and Ágios Górdis. It then becomes more secluded again. The beach at the northern spit between the sea and Lake Chalikúnas is almost completely deserted and the few bathers to the southwest of the lake lose themselves in the expansive, *Sahara-like* dunes of Ágios Geórgios Argirádon. In the extreme south, a

| 1967–1974 | 2002 | 2004 | 2010–2014 | Since 2015 |
|---|---|---|---|---|
| Military dictatorship followed by democracy | The euro replaces the drachma as the national currency | The Olympic Games are held in Athens | Greece can only be saved from national bankruptcy through strict economising, financial aid from the European Union and the International Monetary Fund | A radical left-wing coalition under the leadership of Aléxis Tsipras rules |

What could be nicer than to end the day on one of Kérkyra's restaurant terraces?

noisy counterpoint is provided by Kávos with its narrow strips of sand where there is an *all-day party* and plenty of close contact on the beach.

A stroll through the *inland villages* is also highly recommended. Mountain bikes are only suitable for the fittest however as many of the narrow lanes are like roller coasters with the road between Áno Korakianá and Sokráki resembling a corkscrew.

The most striking feature on a drive through the island's inland is the blanket of *olive trees.* Many of the trees are several centuries old and have been tended since Venetian times to supply Venice with oil for its lanterns, frying pans and salad bowls. There are reportedly

> **Many olive trees are several hundred years old**

4.5 million olive trees on Corfu. Nearly every village on the island, and there are over 100 in total, has its own press and olives are mainly pressed between November and March. The *village squares* are a hive of activity whatever the time of year. Locals gather here in the morning and late afternoon to watch the comings and goings. If you stick around for longer than 15 minutes, you will surely get talking to the locals. And if they don't start talking to you, a trick is to ask them the way somewhere – anywhere!

# WHAT'S HOT

## 1 Daring men

**Women like well-styled men** and increasingly more Greek males are responding by asking their barber for a "pompadour undercut" or "man bun". While their British counterparts are left wondering what is meant, it seems the whole of Corfu is a catwalk for fashionable haircuts. The best hair stylists in Kérkyra work by appointment only. *Michális Vitouladítis (Odós E. Voulgaréos 65 | New Town | tel. 26 61 02 73 22 | www.michalisv.gr)* offers a "hair & scalp therapy" but don't worry there's no scalping involved. Male grooming costs around 15 euros and leaves every man feeling great. All hairdressers and barbers speak English so you won't come out looking a disaster. A good address is *Celebrity (Odós Mitr. Methodíou | New Town | tel. 26 61 02 32 86)* with a nail studio next door for women while their men are transformed into the next Adonis.

## Lucrative students

*Tsipourádika* Students are known for having little spare cash. However they spend more money in cafés and tavernas than most all-inclusive holidaymakers. Increasingly more establishments are responding by catering for the 4000 students and their young lecturers at the Ionian University. The current hotspots are the small pubs called *tsipourádika* in the narrow lane Prosaléndou behind the Old Port. The pubs along this stretch offer great food and entertainment for just 12 euros such as *To Aláto-Pipéri (Odós Dóna 17/Prosaléndou)*, *Bakalogátos (Odós Alypou 23/ Prosaléndou)* or *Alchimiká Gliká (Odós Prosaléndou 16)*.

# Better wines

*Red or white?* Once the only question to be asked when ordering a Corfiot wine. Today, Corfu's wine growers have become real wine producers and seven wineries now bottle wines which they venture to sell outside Corfu *(www.e-corfu.com)*. When asked his favourite tipple in the film "For Your Eyes Only", James Bond stated a preference for the white wine from the *Theotoky Estate (Mon–Sat by appointment only | tel. 69 45 53 90 16 | www.theotoky.com)* at Giannádes. This is an exclusive estate which even has vintage wines in its cellar. A more rustic, down-to-earth address for winetasting is *Livadiotis (any time if someone is there)* close to the Gardíki castle. Vassilikí Karoúnou has added a restaurant to her vineyard *Ambelónas (June–Oct Wed–Fri 7pm–11pm, Dec–May Sun 1pm–6pm | www.ambelonas-corfu.gr)* near Pélekas where you can taste Corfiot specialities to accompany your wines.

# Websites are out

*Online information* Although websites on Corfu are usually creative in design, they often lack up-to-date information and news. Admittedly it's hard work maintaining a homepage which is why many of Corfu's restaurant and café owners have switched to Facebook & co for posting events and live acts. Hoteliers prefer to pay commission fees to booking.com and airbnb.com rather than engaging the services of professional web agencies. More and more private Facebook accounts are also being created. Simply enter "corfu" or "kérkyra" into your browser and the list of results is endless.

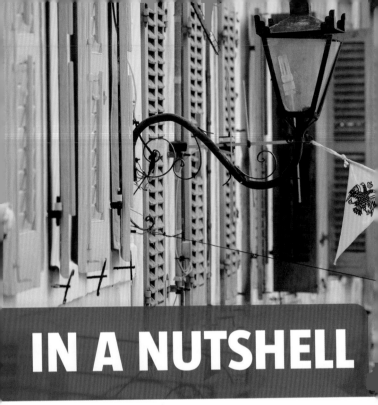

# IN A NUTSHELL

## BANKS & BUILDING BOOM

Before the country was declared bankrupt in 2010, many Greeks were living in a land of milk and honey. Their banks would call regularly trying to sell them a loan. "What, only 20,000 euros? No chance, take 50,000", the banks would say, knowing full well who owned what land and how much money their clients earned. New building developments were then proposed, making people believe they had sufficient financial means to invest. Many people unfortunately succumbed to temptation: the roads are full of large luxury limousines, SUVs and off-roaders as well as many unfinished buildings. The banks' generosity stopped as soon as the crisis hit. The Greeks are now in serious debt. The only compensation is that the banks cannot find buyers for houses they want to put up for auction.

## CORFU PHILHARMONICS

Forget the blasting sounds from the island's beach clubs; Corfu looks back on a long musical tradition. Every larger town has its own philharmonic society, which offers music lessons for children either for free or at an affordable cost. You can often hear them practising when you walk by. To see the full effect, the young players often participate in marching bands and other public parades. Some of the philharmonic orchestras also take part in international guest performances. Admittedly, classical music is not every-

Corfu is different from your usual surroundings, which you'll notice quite soon. Get to know why that is the case

man's taste. Guitars are often hanging in tavernas for guests to play. The traditional, almost Neapolitan sounding kantádes can still sometimes be heard on the island while a more popular sound is the traditional *rembétiko*. These protest songs dating from the 1920s and 1930s have seen a revival since the financial crisis with contemporary reinterpretations. *Rembétika* are also played in discos and clubs along with hits from the Scorpions or other heavy metal bands. The island is also the birthplace of two Eurovision

Song Contest performers; Vicky Leandros who represented Luxembourg in 1972 as well as the more famous Sakis Rouvas, who successfully performed for Greece in 2004 and 2009 with "Shake It", Greece's best-selling song.

## DROPPING OUT OR ADOPTING A NEW LIFESTYLE

After a holiday on Corfu, many people dream of settling permanently on the island. Currently, around 900 Brits live here

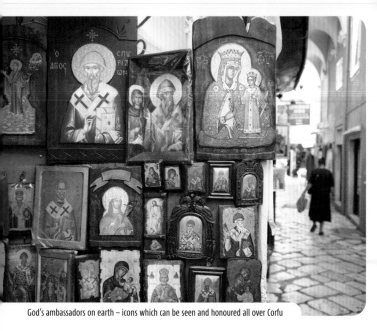

God's ambassadors on earth – icons which can be seen and honoured all over Corfu

and many other nationalities. As long as the foreigners spend money and don't try to open up a shop or pub, they are welcomed by the Corfiots. If they try to compete with the locals, they can count on regular official inspections and even damage to their property. Only those who are really innovative and provide something that is completely new have a chance of being accepted. One good example of a family who has succeeded is the Kalkmanns in Afiónas. They buy olive oil from regional farmers and fill it into attractive packaging; a win-win situation for both parties.

# ECONOMIC CRISIS

The Greek people have been forced to carry the heavy burden of Greece's economic and financial crisis and the country's sovereign debt. Salaries, pensions and social benefits have all been cut while taxes rose considerably. Youth unemployment has reached over 50 percent while the country's general rate of unemployment has exceeded 25 percent – and there are no real signs of recovery. Even a radical incision (i.e. debt relief) will not prevent this patient surviving off the euro cash lifeline from its European neighbours. The Corfiots have adapted their lifestyle accordingly. They are planting vegetables instead of ornamental shrubs, only ordering what they can eat in tavernas, buying smaller cars and have stopped building new houses. They are also giving each other a helping hand rather than relying on day workers from Eastern Europe. As long as the tourists keep coming, they will manage to survive.

# HOISTING THE FLAG

Most Corfiots are obsessed with flags. And in Europe they are not alone.

Two flags in particular are held in high regard. The white and blue flag stands for the Greek nation and not just the Greek State which nobody really likes. This traditional flag can be seen flattering in the wind outside buildings and is also kept inside many Greek homes for special occasions. The latest craze sweeping through Greece are even trainers sporting the flag. The second flag is the black, Byzantine double eagle on a yellow background which represents the former greatness of Greece but is in fact the flag of Constantinople, known since 1453 as Istanbul. Some Greek revolutionaries would like to see a return to this period. Many football fans also like to wave the flags of their favourite teams: red and white are the colours of Olympiakos Piräus, a type of Hellenic Manchester United. Like most Greek island residents, many Corfiots support this team from the Port of Athens. The number 7 is painted on many house facades, street walls and traffic signs which stands for the stadium gate no. 7 where only the most dedicated (and wildest) fans conjugate in the stadium of Piräus. The main rival from Athens, Panathinaikós, is represented with the number 13.

## LAND OF CONFUSION

Corfiots are quite liberal where their spelling is concerned, a custom which can confuse many a tourist. In Greek place names can be written differently on signs and maps while the Latin spelling is even more haphazard. "Agios" meaning "Saint" is a good example. It is sometimes written as "Agios" (as in the Marco Polo guides) or "Aghios" or even "Ayios". All three spellings are accepted and combined as the Greeks please.
But that's not all: things get even more confusing on entering villages. Although most places use house numbers, they are rarely marked on buildings and even the village locals don't know them. The business of matrimony is also not quite so straightforward: it is the liberal custom of married women not to accept their husband's name but instead to retain their maiden name only. They also often refer to their husband as simply their *zissigós,* their life partner. Although for some it is a welcome break with tradition, for others (especially tourists) it can get awfully confusing.

## LOTTERY TICKET SELLERS & BETTING FEVER

Corfiots are crazy about sport. Even in rural villages without tourists, a football or basketball game is always showing on one of the flat screens in the *kafenía* and bars. This obsession with sport has little to do with athletic prowess or enthusiasm: the state-owned OPAP bookmakers have thousands of agencies throughout Greece and are to blame for the Greek's foible for gambling. You will also encounter the socially deprived wandering the streets selling tickets and scratch cards for the three major national lottery companies. Even betting office licences are awarded based on social aspects. Greek Olympic champions sometimes also receive a license to secure them real gold.

## MULTICULTURAL

Globalisation has also not overlooked this small island. Foreigners have always played an important role in determining Corfu's destiny, formerly as rulers with the Corfiots as their helpers. Now life is changing on Corfu. The olive harvest would be impossible without day labourers from Albania and there would be even more fish in the sea without the help of fishermen from the Nile Delta. Many houses would remain unbuilt and many hotel rooms uncleaned without Bulgarian and Romanian muscle power. In former times only Romani people made their way through the villages with their laden-down carts. Today people from Southeast Asia in Korean cars complement this with electronic goods and Africans specialise in illicitly pressed CDs and DVDs. Even the evening entertainment would be less interesting without foreigners. Many hotels and beach bars hire multi-lingual Czechs and Hungarians for their animation programmes.

## NEVER ALONE

Corfiots do not like spending time on their own. A cosy twosome is also reserved for a certain hour of the day. Otherwise Greeks prefer a *paréa*; a group of friends or acquaintances, who regularly meet up to drink coffee or eat, go to the disco and on holiday together. The question asked by friends afterwards is not what the hotel or food was like but how the *paréa* was. In case you do have to go it alone, you will always be accom-

panied by the island's saints. They are present as icons wherever you go on the island – whether in the car, in the ticket booth or in the fields – either as printed images or painted on church and chapel walls and hanging on the sides of the road. You know you are always in safe hands and in good company.

## ORGANIC FARMERS AND OLIVE GROVES

There are actually many farmers on Corfu who would like to produce organic goods with better prospects for sales and higher prices – especially for wine and olive oil. However, the hurdles are too high as it is difficult for them to keep the minimum distance from the fields and groves of "chemical farmers" and there is still no press on the island that exclusively processes organically grown olives. Despite no eco labelling, you can be sure the oil is of a good and healthy quality. At least, extensive insecticide spraying from the air has been stopped so that each farmer can decide whether to use chemicals or rely on a natural fertilizer

# FAMILY AND OTHER ANIMALS

Any fan of British comedy dramas will surely have seen the ITV series "The Durrells". First broadcast in 2016, it is set on Corfu and has already attracted crowds of new tourists to the island. The series is based on the famous Durrell family: Lawrence was a successful novelist while his younger brother Gerald founded Jersey zoo and was a broadcaster and naturalist for the BBC. Both brothers spent some of their youth with their extravagant mother on Corfu and Gerald wrote about his

experiences in the highly entertaining book "My Family and Other Animals". It offers an amusing insight into the fauna of Corfu, not the first destination on your mind when you think of an island safari yet the island's flamingos are a spectacular sight. They migrate to the salt lake at Lefkími between October and May and can be spotted standing majestically on one leg, the typical posture for these pink-feathered birds.

The nets are in position, the olive harvest can begin

using manure placed in bags under trees to gently drain the rainwater into the soil.

## PLANNING – WHAT'S THAT?!

Do you know what tomorrow will bring? Do as the Corfiots do and don't waste your time planning for the long term. Large events and festivals are only made public a few days in advance while timetables or the opening times of museums or excavation sites are posted online at short notice. Vague arrangements to meet the following morning, afternoon, evening or even next week are made, adding the all-important "ta leme" – "we'll talk again later." You can then expect a call one hour beforehand to confirm the exact time – give or take the customary half hour.

## UNLUCKY ROYALS

Corfu was once a paradise for European royal families. Sisi, the Empress of Austria, and Wilhelm II, the German Kaiser, both owned a small castle here while the Palaia Anaktora housed the Kings of Greece. Prince Philip, the husband of Queen Elizabeth II, was even born on the island. However none of these royals enjoyed a happy end: Sisi was assassinated while Wilhelm was forced to abdicate. Constantine II, the last monarch in Greece, also had to pay off tax debts by selling his palace on Corfu. Philip's mother suffered from schizophrenia and Phillip himself left the island to become the consort of Queen Elizabeth II. This wealthy aristocrat has not completely severed his ties with the island: he chooses to anonymously buy old noble estates on Corfu. In contrast, the Russian billionaire and owner of Chelsea football club, Roman Abramovich, cannot hide his presence; his mega yachts are a clear giveaway. He occasionally resides at his exclusive estate situated at the bay of Dassiá and anchors off the coast of Boukári to eat in his favourite fish restaurant. The owner only has good things to say about the Russian tycoon: "Roman is extremely friendly and very modest."

# FOOD & DRINK

Corfiots would prefer to stay at home rather than eat alone or as a couple. A meal can only be fully enjoyed with the right *paréa*, one single Greek word to mean a group of family or friends gathering together to enjoy each other's company. It can take some time to round up all the guests which is one reason why most Greeks rarely eat before 9pm.

The *paréa* is one way to put the chef's mood to the test. Nobody orders just food for himself and certainly not before quizzing the waiter about what is on today's menu. There is not a set sequence of menu courses as we know it; waiters serve dishes to the table as soon as they are ready in the kitchen and you will only find written menus in touristy restaurants. *Greeks eat mezedákia*, a wide variety of specialities on as many plates as possible.

Most waiters are casually dressed and they start by covering the linen tablecloth with a paper one. Children are invited to scribble on it and nobody feels the need to hide the first food stains under a napkin. A medium-sized plate is decked for each guest, cutlery and serviettes are taken from the obligatory bread basket and guests help themselves to water, wine or beer. A toast is then made to the good company around the table with *jámas* meaning "for our health".

The waiter places all the dishes in the middle of the table. *Everybody takes what* – and as much as they want. Fish and meat are usually served on large

You can eat gyros at home, so here you should try real Corfiot cuisine – usually late at night and hardly ever alone

platters and everyone helps themselves. All the plates, even the empty ones, are left on the table. The waiters don't take any away so that the *paréa* can see how well they dined.

Desserts are brought out at the latest with the bill (which is paid by one person) and are often served on the house with a round of *tsípouro*, a good-quality brandy similar to the Italian grappa. Where's the Oúzo? you might ask. On Corfu, oúzo is rarely drunk after the meal. It is usually enjoyed as an aperitif

or during the meal. Once you have been given your change, a tip can be left on the table on leaving the restaurant. But if you are not invited to join a *paréa*, don't worry – you need not starve. Lone diners and couples are welcomed everywhere and at *most times of the day and night*. Nearly all restaurants and tavernas that don't survive solely from tourism serve warm meals throughout the day, from a proper English breakfast first thing in the morning until midnight. Only occasionally do some restaurants

# LOCAL SPECIALITIES

**bakaljáros me skordaljá** – dried hake *(merluza)* with a potato-garlic puree

**bekri mezé** – pork stewed in red wine

**bourdéto** – Corfiot fish or (sometimes) meat dish in a light, spicy sauce. As a starter, usually prepared with *galéo* (houndshark), or with *skórpios* (scorpion fish) or *pastanáka* (stingray) as a main course

**briám** – a kind of ratatouille

**chélia** – eel, grilled or in aspic: a Corfiot speciality (order in advance)

**gópes** – grilled or fried sardines, often served as a snack

**juvétsi** – noodle gratin with beef (occasionally, with lamb)

**kokorétsi** – grilled offal wrapped in natural skin

**marídes** – crisp, fried anchovies eaten head and all (photo right)

**nouboúlo** – speciality from the northwest of the island: lightly smoked pork (starter)

**pastitsáda** – beef and chicken with noodles

**patsária** – beetroot; cold as a salad or warm as a vegetable dish

**sofríto** – beef, marinated in garlic and vinegar and braised in wine

**spanakópitta** – puff pastry filled with spinach (photo left)

**stifádo** – beef or rabbit stew in a tomato-cinnamon sauce

**táramosaláta** – red puree of potatoes, soaked bread and fish roe (starter)

**tirópitta** – puff pastry filled with cheese

**tzizimbírra** – lemonade with a touch of ginger

close between 4 and 6pm. You are also not restricted to *traditional Greek pubs* known as *mezedopolío, tsipourádiko* or *ouzerí*. The city and all holiday resorts have a wide selection of *restaurants serving international cuisine,* from pizzerias and souvlaki grills to Indian, Chinese and Italian. There are even English

pubs on the gastronomic scene serving traditional pub grub.

Snack bars, *psistariá,* are a good alternative to restaurants for a quick bite. Standing up or sitting down, you can order chicken or pork *gýros* in *pita* bread or on a plate *(mérida)*, meatballs, local sausage and – quite often

– chicken. Chips on the side are omnipresent.

Those with a sweet tooth will make their way to the *zácharoplastío*, the Greek pastry shop, with its mainly oriental specialities such as *baklavás* and *kataífi* ("angel's hair") along with cream and sponge cakes.

Mineral water will always be brought to the table with every meal, and in villages a good-quality tap water or even fresh spring water. *Wine from the barrel is available everywhere* and many restaurant owners are proud of their extensive wine menus with a wide selection of Greek bottled wines. Retsína, the white resonated wine, is not very popular on Corfu. The famous aniseed schnapps, oúzo, competes with the subtle tsípouro to be the favourite tipple among locals.

The Corfiot speciality  *tzitzimbírra* is a non-alcoholic drink made of lemon juice, sugar, water and a touch of ginger. You can sample this from the beginning of May in villages in the interior such as Sokráki in the north of the island. It almost disappeared in the early 1990s but the demand created by the holidaymakers led to the traditional drink remaining on the market. If you order it, you are helping to preserve a tradition – and it is very tasty.

The Greeks *drink coffee* at any time of the day. However, ordering it in Greece is something of a science. You have the choice between a small cup of Greek coffee, *kafé ellenikó*, hot instant coffee, usually called *ness sestó*, cold, whipped instant coffee served with ice cubes, *frappé*, and the trendy *freddo* as either cappuccino or espresso. If you order Greek coffee, you must always say *how sweet you want it* because the ground coffee is mixed with sugar and then brewed: *skétto* is without, *métrio* with a little and *glikó* with a lot of

A good Greek coffee to wake the senses

sugar. And, of course, Greek coffee is *always without milk*. If you want to have your hot or cold Nescafe with milk you just have to add *mä gala*. On Corfu, the older people like to put a small shot of oúzo in their coffee and order *kafé ellinikó mä polí lígo úso mässa*.

**29**

# SHOPPING

Small shopkeepers have successfully survived the onslaught of supermarkets on the island. Only food retailers are feeling the pressure from big name discounters and the traditional one-euro shops are suffering from the large number of Chinese bric-a-brac shops with red lanterns in front.

Village shops are still run by local families, usually with an old lady or man sat behind the counter. The local directory lists no fewer than 20 shoe stores and 34 jewellers in the town of Corfu alone. There are plenty of stores to spend your money in, none of which will blow your holiday budget. On the whole however, the selection of stores is rather conventional with a lack of wow factor. Shoes are the only items to follow the latest fashion trends. Most of the arts and crafts for sale are made in Greece and Corfu with some Greek art also available to buy. And Corfu's plethora of culinary specialities will spoil any well-intentioned diet plans.

*Opening hours:* Shops are usually open from 8:30am to 2pm from Monday to Saturday and from 6pm to 9pm on Tuesday, Thursday and Friday. Most su-

permarkets and souvenir shops are open from 8:30am to 11pm.

## ARTS & CRAFTS

Objects carved out of olive wood are really special: bowls, cups, salad servers, as well as small pieces of furniture such as stools and tables. You can find them in several shops in the Old Town of Corfu and in mountain villages including Makrádes, Lákones and Strinílas as well as the beach resort Acharávi. The best place to buy artistic glassware made on Corfu for your home is in Ágios Stéfanos Avliotón or in the Old Town of Corfu where there are also several antique shops.

Driftwood items are currently in trend such as decorative ships with sails made of faded jeans. Corfiot pottery is always a favourite among tourists whether for decorative or household use.

## CUMQUATS

Cumquats, or *koum kouáts* in Greek – little oranges, a maximum of 4 cm long, with a yellow-orange skin – are a unique island speciality. The vitamin-rich citrus fruit is made into marmalade and liquor or sold

Nature provides the very best things – if you look around, you will discover delicious Corfiot specialities and beautiful arts and crafts

as candied fruit. The latest trend is a newly-created eau de toilette with a fruity, tangy cumquat aroma.

## HONEY

Treat your breakfast guests back home to honey from Corfu or give your dishes an authentic Greek taste by adding some of the island's dried herbs. Greek walnuts or a honey-sesame bar also offer the ideal in-between snack.

## MUSIC

Many souvenir shops sell CDs with Greek music à la Alexis Zorba at reasonable prices – although no Greek would ever buy them. If you are looking for good recordings of up-to-date Greek music of any kind, you should visit the special shops in the island's capital where you will get good advice and be able to listen to the music.

## OLIVE OIL

Pure olive oil from Corfu tastes even better if you know which grove it has come from. However, the security standards now in force when you are flying mean that you should only buy it in cans. Another delicious Corfiot speciality is olive paste – great as a dip or spread on bread.

## WINE, LIQUEURS & SPIRITS

You can taste Corfiot wines, liqueurs and spirits in cellars and distilleries, as well as roadside booths before you buy them. However, it is usually difficult to transport wine. You can also choose to have Corfiot wines (and other local products) delivered to your doorstep by ordering them via the *www.e-corfu.com* homepage, although the shipping rates are a bit on the expensive side.

# CORFU TOWN

**WHERE TO START?**
To reach the central Esplanade (U E–F 3–5) (*m e–f 3–5*), go up to Plátia G. Theotókou (Sarocco Square) from the long-distance bus terminal. This is also the terminus for busses to the nearby beaches. The Odós G. Theotóki that makes its way as Odós Voulgaréos through the Old Town will lead you to the open square between the Old Fortress, Old Palace and Ionian Academy. It is best to park your car at the Old Port (the Esplanade car park is often full) and then walk through the Old Town or along the sea.

**MAP INSIDE BACK COVER**

No matter where you are based on the island, it's worth visiting the town of Corfu (Greek: Kérkyra) (135 E5–6) (*m D5*) at least twice. Here you can explore the authentic side of Greece where the ancient meets the modern. Standing directly on the island's coast, this fun city has a lot to offer with something new to discover at every turn.

You will need a morning to stroll through the market and shopping district and visit the museums, churches and forts followed by a spot of shopping and eating. Finish your first day chilling out by the sea at one of the many beach bars. For your second visit to the city, return in the late afternoon to wander along the Es-

## World Heritage Site Kérkyra – a lively metropolis whose Old Town is considered the most beautiful in the country

planade, try one of the many types of coffee under the shady arcades, take a horse-drawn carriage ride through the old town and enjoy a sundowner while watching the sunset over the Corfu skyline. Meet the locals for an evening meal before immersing yourself in the Greek nightlife. The choice of music is entirely up to you.

Corfu (pop. 28,000) is a cosmopolitan city. Imbued with Venetian, British and French influences while tainted by Serbian and German past, the heart of Corfu has remained Greek despite the influx of foreign visitors. The Corfiots are a discrete yet friendly folk. The elegant arcades are bursting with rows of shops which line the wide lanes with their marble paving. All over the town small squares appear dotted with cafés. Imposing Italian-style red-dome clock towers soar above five and six-storey century-old houses where washing lines stretch from balcony to balcony especially in the Old Town district *Cambiéllo*.

Friendly dogs and cats roam the lanes and red-brick walls show behind the crumbling render. An old archway can be seen here and there while decorative reliefs and statues adorn the walls of other dilapidated houses. The former Jewish quarter is home to one of Europe's oldest synagogues and you will also spot buildings decorated with the Star of David.

Corfu's Old Town is the perfect place to wander and visit the entertaining mu-

The Old Fortress withstood many sieges; today, it is the symbol of Kérkyra

seums and panoramic castles. If you're looking to escape the city for more tranquil and green surroundings, catch the city bus to Mon Repos to visit Greece's most beautiful park followed by Kanóni from where you can ferry over to "Mouse Island", the favourite spot of Empress Sisi. Her former residence, by the way, is easily and cheaply reached by bus.

## SIGHTSEEING

### AGÍAS EFTHÍMIAS CONVENT
(135 E6) (*𝒲 D5*)

This tranquil Venetian convent is the perfect spot for a spot of meditative respite between Corfu's major attractions. Although situated in the town, Agía Efímia is a tiny, idyllic location away from the crowds of tourists and particularly notable for its beautiful flower-filled courtyard. The nuns open up their convent to the public and may even serve you a cup of Greek coffee…. *In summer daily 8am–1pm and 5–8pm; at other times 9am–noon and 4–6pm | Anemómilos | on the road from Mon Repos beach to the Paleópils Basilica*

### ÀGIOS SPIRÍDONAS CHURCH ●
(U E2–3) (*𝒲 e2–3*)

Believers have showered the church of the island's patron saint, which is located in the centre of the Old Town, with votive offerings. Its most precious relics are the bones of St Spiridon, a Cypriot martyr from around 300 AD. A noble Corfiot family purchased his remains from a travelling salesman in 1456, as was common all over Europe in medieval times. Over the centuries the relics have not only blessed the common folk; they have saved entire cities, islands and countries from war and helped to contain the spread of the pest and cholera. Saint Spyridon also exceeded all expectations when he was attributed to saving Corfu from the hands of the Turks in 1716. He still attracts many followers and believers even today.

Believers of all age groups come throughout the day, light a candle, kiss the sarcophagus and write their wishes or thanks to the saint in a book. Silver oil lamps, donated by believers, hang over the sarcophagus. It is easy to recognise that some of them were donated by seamen and ship owners: they are decorated with silver model boats or with votive plates of ship reliefs. Take a seat in the nave on the right to watch the comings and goings. *Open during the day | Odós Spirídonos*

### ARCHEOLOGICAL MUSEUM ★
(U B6) (*Ⓜ b6*)

The sight of the horrifying visage of the gorgon Medusa is enough to give anyone a fright. This ancient Greek creature has snakes growing out of her hair and shoulders and hanging around her waist. Her googly eyes appear to be popping out of her head, her tongue is hanging out of her wide mouth. No wonder that the Ancient Greeks believed the sight of her turned the enemy to stone and had this gorgon erected on the gable of their most important temple to ward off thieves and fire.

The museum also exhibits more attractive artefacts: Dionysus, the God of wine and theatre, is engraved into a second smaller gable as well as several majes-

---

★ **Archaeological Museum**
Masterpieces of early Greek art, unfortunately being restored → p. 35

★ **Byzantine Museum**
Narrative icons exhibited in an old church building → p. 36

★ **Esplanade**
A beautiful open space with many pavement cafés → p. 37

★ **Mon Repos**
A small castle in an overgrown park → p. 39

★ **Old Fortress Café**
Cool design, drinks and tasty snacks in the historic fortress → p. 43

★ **Vassilákis**
Corfiot liqueurs and spirits → p. 44

★ **Weekly Market**
Held in the moat of the Old Fortress → p. 44

★ **Roof Garden Cavalieri**
An evening spent above the roofs of the town → p. 46

★ **Imabári**
The city's nicest beach bar, day and night → p. 46

★ **Achíllion**
German-Austrian fairy-tale castle high above the sea with a magnificent garden → p. 47

**MARCO POLO HIGHLIGHTS**

tic lions. One of the lions dates from the early archaic period around 630 BC and is believed to be the first sculpture of a lion in all of Europe.

*New opening times (unknown at the time of going to press) | Odós Wraíla 1*

INSIDER TIP **BRITISH CEMETERY**
**(U A–B6) (ⓜ a–b6) ●**
The cemetery with its colonial tombstones seems like an enchanted park and it is not only a romantic place but also a great attraction for flower-lovers in spring and autumn with its many wild orchids. *Daily, from sunrise to sunset | Odós Kolokotróni 25*

## BYZANTINE MUSEUM ★
**(U D1) (ⓜ d1)**
More than 100 valuable icons from the 15th–18th centuries from Corfiot houses of worship have found a dignified new home in the *Panagía Antivuniótissa* Church in the Old Town. Soft Byzantine music can be heard in the background while you make your visit. Of the stories these icons tell, two are especially noteworthy. The fourth icon on the left after the cash desk, a traditional Byzantine icon from around 1490, shows St George on a horse with a young boy holding a teapot and cup sitting behind him (no. 186). Pirates had abducted him and made him their cupbearer. In her sorrow, his mother turned to St George who brought her son back to her. The icon to the left of the west portal is a work by the famous Cretan painter Michaíl Damáskinos from around 1752 in the so-called Cretan style, showing Saints Sérgios, Bákchos and Justini (no. 141). It is felt that they were responsible for the Christian fleet defeating the Turks on their feast day, 7 October, in 1571. They are shown standing on a decapitated three-headed monster symbolising the Turkish fleet.

The life icons portray the hagiography (or vita) of Saint Nicholas telling a series of miracles he performed (no. 186). In dif-

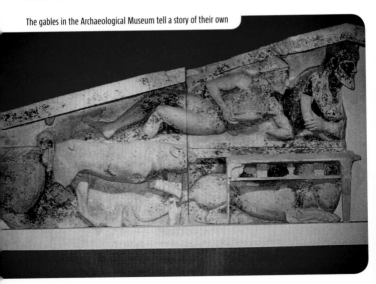

The gables in the Archaeological Museum tell a story of their own

ferent ten scenes, he rescues people at sea, stops the sword of a hangman who wants to execute an innocent man and offers a bag full of money to a poor father who is forced to put his daughter up for prostitution. *Tue–Sun 9am–4pm | admission 3.50 euros, combined ticket 8 euros | steps lead up from Odós Arseníu*

## CAMBIÉLLO (U E–F 3–5) (*ℳ e–f 3–5*)

Put away your Marco Polo guide now and enjoy an aimless stroll between the sea promenade, Odós Filéllinon, Odós Ágios Spirídonos and the Old Palace through the old town's most beguiling district. Pass by the local stray cats and dogs, walk under the washing lines stretched from window to window and meet the locals who live here. There is no store or *kafenío* around here to distract you. It is purely a residential area where students have found affordable accommodation on the top floors of dilapidating houses and old people are content with gazing down at the streets below because most of the buildings are without lifts. The district is proof that beauty can emerge from poverty and leaves you dreaming of which one of the penthouse flats in the century-old five and six-storey buildings you would renovate if you had the money.

The ● ★ *Esplanade* is a hive of activity. The broad expanse of the Esplanade is the centre of all social life, the site of the *vólta* – the traditional promenade held every evening – and occasional military parades; it is a meeting place for young and old, for the locals and holidaymakers. The Venetians created it in the 17th century. Until then, the houses in the town reached all the way to the Old Fortress. The army had them torn down to have the unrestricted possibility to open fire in the case of a siege. Later, this green area was used as a pa-

Enchanted and peaceful: the British Cemetery

rade ground but today cricket is played on the grass. There is a fountain in the shady park. One of the monuments erected here commemorates the unification of the Ionian Islands with free Greece in 1864. It shows seven bronze reliefs with symbols of the seven main islands. Corfu is represented by the ship of the Phaeacians, the legendary people that – according to Homer – lived on Corfu and brought Odysseus back to his homeland of Ithaca by ship.

The west side of the Esplanade is flanked by tall, 19th-century houses that are still lived in today. It is lovely to sit in the little armchairs in one of the cafés under their arcades or *liston* – although it is quite pricey.

A cheaper alternative is to picnic on the other side, to the left of the entrance of the Old Fort. In the Boschetto park, a table and chairs made from palm tree stumps invite guests to take a picnic surrounded by onlookers. From here it is just a few steps to the horse-drawn carriages which line up waiting to take you on a 40-minute tour of the city. Afterwards, you can head up to the rooftop garden bar of the Hotel Cavalieri in the south-west corner of the Esplanade to take in the amazing views of Corfu at night.

### CASA PARLANTE ● (U E3) *(🗺 e3)*

Seeing is believing! This "talking house" in the old town invites you to visit the former home of a noble Corfiot family from around 1830. Tours are organised by a friendly young group of guides who first introduce you to the family members – all animated figures: The father is reading international newspapers, the mother is drinking some of the finest English tea and the children are practising the piano and violin under the watchful eye of their strict governess. You are invited to a glass of liqueur and sweet pastry while taking in the building's sounds and smells. The tour ends by descending into the cramped living quarters of the servants and kitchen. You will return to the 21st century after about 30 minutes. *Daily 10am–8pm | admission 5 euros | Odós N. Theotóki 16 | www.casaparlante.gr*

### FALIRÁKI (ÁGIOS NIKÓLAS GATE) (U F1) *(🗺 f1)*

Today, the lovely building with the small St Nicholas Chapel on a peninsula north of the Old Fortress is an ideal place to relax on the waterfront with a drink or have a delicious meal. In the 19th century, this was where those travelling by the steam and sailing-ships anchored at the docks, which was often where emigrants departed for America, went on board or disembarked. *Usually 8pm–2am (as long as the bars are open) | free access from Odós Arseníu*

### KÁNONI, VLACHÉRNA MONASTERY AND PONTIKONÍSSI ● ☼ (135 E6) *(🗺 D 5–6)*

From the panoramic terrace at Kanóni, why not film one of the planes from the airline you arrived on by take-off or landing? This will make an entertaining addition to your holiday album. The phenomenal view of the airport and planes is not the only spectacular sight from this lookout point. Turn 90° to see Corfu's favourite postcard image: the small islands of *Vlachérna* and *Pontikoníssi* off the coast which you probably brushed over during your descent by plane. You can get even closer by reaching over a small causeway which is almost entirely taken up by the monastery that was built around 1700 – now no longer in use. Boats set out from the causeway to the "Mouse Island" (the translation of Pontikoníssi) where Austria's Empress "Sisi" liked to sit. The small church was built in the 12th century. *Monastery and church open to the public during the day | city bus line 2*

### KÍPOS TOU LAOÚ (U F2) *(🗺 f2)*

What do Ground Zero and the "public gardens" to the south of the Old Palace have in common? Both memorial sites invite visitors to touch the plaques and commemorate the tragic loss of lives. In New York, you can tenderly touch a bronze panel with the names of the 9-11 victims while on Corfu you can stroke the feather-like wings of the statue, which was erected in memory of the 280 Italian officers who were murdered and drowned (by weighing the corpses with rocks) by the German mountain infantry in 1943.

## MON REPOS ★ (135 E6) (*DD D5*)

A little known fact is that Prince Phillip of Greece, who was to marry Queen Elizabeth II, was once pushed around the enchanting grounds of Mon Repos in his pushchair. Born in this small castle on 10 June 1921, there is nothing here to remind you that his family once resided here; the Palazzo now houses a colour collection of memorabilia connected to the island's history and flora. The visit is not mandatory but you probably won't get another chance to take such a leisurely half-hour INSIDER TIP park stroll anywhere else in Greece. Covered in ivy, most of these tropical trees are almost 200 years old.

The remains of two Ancient Greek temples are also dotted around the gardens, the ● *Doric Temple* is ideal for a few peaceful moments sitting in the grass or picnicking between the 2500-year old pillars. *Park daily 8am–7pm | admission free | museum Tue–Fri 8:30am–3pm | admission 3 euros | entrance at the Paleópolis stop on the bus route to Kanóni.*

## NEW FORT (NÉO FRÚRIO) ✷ (U A–B 2–3) (*DD a–b 2–3*)

All good things come in threes. Even if you have already seen the old town of Corfu from the Old Fort and the Cavalieri roof garden, you may still like to climb up the New Fort. The *New Fort* is not at all new, only not quite as old as the Old Fort. The Venetians built it in the 16th century. You will be rewarded with a stylish café on the top of the fortress walls, rarely visited by other tourists. The adventurous among you will also be treated to several small bars and night clubs dotted around the entrance to the fort. You can check out the evening's program when you walk by – maybe there is an insider tip where you will meet locals only. *June–Sept daily, April/May, Oct daily 10am–3pm | admission free | entrance Odós Solomú*

Just a few steps further to reach the end of the monastery island of Vlachérna

## OLD FORT
(U C5–6) (*M c5–6*)

Start your tour of the city at the Old Venetian Fort which offers a great over-view of the city. After that, you'll know your way around! You are treated to splendid views over the whole town if you wander up the first of the two hills on the rocky headland – you can quench your thirst afterwards at the fort's café. Although resembling an Ancient Greek masterpiece, the temple in front of you was in fact built by the British: the former Anglican St. George's Church is modelled on a Doric temple. On leaving the fort, you have views from the bridge over the artificial moat, the *Contrafossa,* which some Corfiots use as their weekend re-treat and keep primitive huts in which they store their barbecues and fishing gear. *May–Oct daily 8am–8pm, Nov–April daily 8am–3pm | admission 4 euros, combined ticket 8 euros, after that, free until 2am – but without access to the peak*

## OLD PALACE
(U F2) (*M f2*)

Take your pick between scenes from "Hello!" or "Playboy" in this museum. Just beyond the northern end of the Esplanade, the Old Palace was built from 1819–23 by Maltese workers using sandstone they had brought over from Malta. The con-struction was commissioned by the British to house their Lord High Commissioner and the three large func-tion rooms facing the Esplanade once hosted parties for the island's British elite and later Greece's Royal Family. The lead-ers of EU countries also held a conference here in 1994, the renovations for which were financed from EU subsidies. Asian art, which was collected by well-off Greeks and offered as gifts to their country, is on display in most of the other rooms. Hidden away in one corner of the muse-um are ● erotic reliefs portraying "acro-batic" Kama Sutra scenes, taken from the famous temple at the Khajuraho Group of Monuments in India. *April–Oct Tue–Sun 8am–7:30pm, at other times 8:30am–3pm | admission 6 euros, com-bined ticket 8 euros | Esplanade*

## PALEÓPOLIS (135 E6) (*M D5*)

Towards the end of the 5th century, the early Christians on Corfu built a church with five naves on top of the, still recognis-able, remains of a small Roman music theatre, an "Odeon", and traces can still be seen in the ground. Its floor was orig-

## LOW BUDGET

You can save money on admission costs with the combined ticket (see p. 124). If you choose the right day – or are in Kérkyra by chance – many of the sights in the town can be visited free of charge. Entrance to the *Byz-antine Museum* (U D1) (*M d1*), the *Old Palace* (U F2) (*M f2*) and the *Old Fort* (U C5–6) (*M c5–6*) is free eve-ry first Sunday each month from No-vember to March, on all public hol-idays, 6 March, the last weekend in September, World Museum Day in May, on World Memorial Day on 18 April and on World Environment Day on 5 June.

Feel like fast food? The greatest choice can be found on the Espla-nade (U E–F4) (*M e–f4*) at the west end of Odós Dousmáni; many typi-cal gyros taverns can be found in the streets parallel to Odós Zaitsainóu near the Old Port (U C2) (*M c2*).

inally decorated with magnificent mosaics and some lovely fragments have been preserved in the exhibition rooms in the Old Fortress. The impressive walls come from a small, Gothic church from the Venetian period that included Antique elements. *Tue–Sun 8am–3pm | admission free | opposite the entrance to the Mon Repos Castle Park | City bus to Kanóni, Paleópolis stop*

## SYNAGOGUE
(U C3) (ℳ c3)

Multiculturalism is nothing new. Corfu has always been a multicultural society. Orthodox Corfiots, Catholic Venetians, bath and the Greek steward is on hand to provide brief explanations in English on request. *Daily 10am–3pm | admission free | Odós Velissáriou 4*

## VÍDOS
(135 E5) (ℳ D5)

Interested in a small boat ride? Then ferry out to the lush, green outcrop of Vídos. There are two ways of reaching the island: an affordable ferry service from the Old Port makes the crossing in just a few minutes. You can walk across the island in 40 minutes following the well-signposted paths to reach a couple of tiny pebble beaches and also discover

The New Fort occupies a hill-top site between the old and new ports

Cretans who fled their homeland from the Turks as well as the French, British and now tourists – the island has been a melting pot of cultures over the centuries. Jews made up a strong part of this population until the Germans came and deported 2000 members of the Jewish community. Only one of the three synagogues has remained standing. This two-storey cult building dating from the 17th century has become a place of silent remembrance commemorating all the victims of the National Socialism. It can be visited every day except on the Sabthat the island is an important pilgrim site for Serbs. Ten thousand Serbian soldiers were quarantined on the island by the enemy troops in World War I and many died of hunger and epidemics. Their descendants erected a memorial on Vídos to commemorate their loved ones.

The island can also be reached by taking the *Calypso Star* which departs from the same jetty at the Old Port. On calm days, passengers can stand in the ship's hull and observe the sea life through large windows while the boat circles the island.

Due to the unpredictability of fish, a sea lion show has also been added to the excursion program – to the objection of animal rights activists! *In summer, small ferries take passengers to and from Vídos from the Old Port, daily 10am–midnight | eturn trip 2.20 euros | Calypso Star every hour 10am–6pm | departure from the same jetty at the Old Port | 15 euros*

## FOOD & DRINK

### AEGLI
(U E2) *(菜 e2)*

Have you ever been invited to dine with a diplomat? The proprietor of this exclusive restaurant is no less than the Honorary Consul of Germany who combines his official title with his gastronomic activities. Although none of the guests wear ties or evening dresses, this fine-dining establishment boasts linen napkins, white tablecloths and a professional service. Table booking is necessary. *Daily | Odós I. Kapodístrias 13 | Esplanade | tel. 26 61 03 19 49 | Expensive*

### INSIDER TIP BELLISSIMO
(U D3) *(菜 d3)*

Father and son, Kóstas and Stávros, take care of the service. Ánna and Dóra are in charge of the kitchen. There are five to six different homemade specialities every day along with gyros and grilled meat. *Spanakópitta,* home made puff pastry filled with chard, mint, leek, a bit of cheese and touch of fennel, is pure poetry. Meals are served on a pretty, newly laid-out, square. *Mon–Sat, in August also Sun evening | Odós D. Bitzárou Kyriaki | entrance between 67 and 69 Odós N. Theotóki | Moderate*

The Esplanade in Kérkyra is atmospheric in the evening

### INSIDER TIP EKTÓS SKÉDIO
(U C2) (*m c2*)

In this appropriately named "no plan" restaurant, the waiter brings to the table a hand-written menu along with an order card where you can enter what you'd like to eat, preferably in Greek but English will do. Your *mezedákia* then arrives in batches of small portions which are placed in the middle of the table for everyone to help themselves. If you run out of food, you can simply ask the waiter for seconds. The Corfiots love to choose what and how they want to eat – free tables are scarce after 10pm. *Mon–Sat only in the evening | Odós Prossaléndiou 43 | behind the Court building | Moderate*

### KÁTHE PRÁMA STON KAIRÓ TOU
(U D2) (*m d2*)

This restaurant is just as unusual as its name meaning "Everything in good time". The landlord Spíros is an artistic chef offering individual interpretations of traditional Greek dishes. His mussels in muscatel are a dream just as the lamb meatballs served on a bed of aubergine puree. *Daily | Odós Mitropóleos 22 | Moderate*

### OLD FORTRESS CAFÉ ★
(U C6) (*m c6*)

The modern café in the Old Fort is an atmospheric location to drink excellent Greek wines, cocktails or *tsípouro* (grappa) accompanied by an omelette, salad, or platter of mixed starters, *pikilies*. There are concerts on some evenings. *Daily | in the Old Fort (see p. 40) | admission only with a valid ticket when the Old Fort is open; after that, free | Expensive*

### PÉRGOLA ☺
(U C3) (*m c3*)

Sákis, the owner of this unpretentious taverna, serves the best Greek food, slightly sparkling wine from the village of Zitsa on the mainland and excellent grappa. Stuffed aubergines with a cheese topping and his salad of wild greens *tsigarélli* are heavenly. *Daily | Odós Agías Sofias 10 | Moderate*

### ROÚVAS
(U C4) (*m c4*)

There is no outdoor seating in this typical market taverna, but here you can choose your meal directly from the pots of – mostly – stewed dishes. The salads are fresh and crisp, and the vegetables and meat come from the market. Many stall holders eat here – they know what quality is! *Mon–Sat 9am–5pm | Odós Dessíla 13 | Budget*

### INSIDER TIP TABERNITA MEXICANA
(U B3) (*m b3*)

Tables and chairs are spread out over several small terraces and lawn areas of this tavern's garden, either in the sun or under the garden's shady trees. The Greek-Canadian couple who own the tavern specialise in excellent steaks and Mexican cuisine but also have pizza and Greek dishes on their menu. Guests are welcome to drink just a coffee, cocktails or a selection of tequilas. *Daily | Odós Solomoú 31 | near the entrance to the New Fort | Moderate*

## SHOPPING

The main shopping streets for the locals are Odós Vuláreos in the Old Town and its continuation, ● Odós G. Theotóki, in the new section with its beautiful arcades. Modern shops, especially those selling electrical items and multimedia, can be found on the wide Odós Aléxandras that runs from Platía G. Theotóki (Sarocco Square) to the sea. Arts and crafts and souvenirs are mainly offered on Odós N. Theotóki, Odós

Filarmonikís and Odós Filéllinon in the Old Town. There alre also many small shops in Odós Ag. Sofías in the old Jewish quarter.

### BLANC DU NIL (U C2) *(𝄞 c2)*

Do you like wearing white? Then you've found your vegan clothing paradise in this boutique: fashionable clothes for both him and her exclusively in white made from the finest Egyptian cotton. You don't have to start planning your wedding though; "white nights" are popular theme nights in many Corfu clubs. *Odós Agíon Pándon 20 | Old Port*

### INSIDER TIP BY TOM ● 🌐
(U C2) *(𝄞 c2)*

Are you fed up with all the plastic in your kitchen? If so, Thomás Koumarákos is your man. Thomás still only uses traditional techniques and has been putting his heart and soul into his work since he started in 1969. He makes everything from chopping boards, salad servers and bowls to egg cups. Visitors will enjoy the endearing smell of wood from his workshop and his collection of tools is no less impressive. He revels in making bespoke pieces for his customers – within a few hours and at a reasonable price. *Parodós N. Theotóki 3i | entrance between the houses at 81 and 83 Odós N. Theotóki*

### CELDES
(U C2) *(𝄞 c2)*

Greece at, or even, on your feet? On a footprint of just 5 m$^2$/54 sq. ft, this store specialises in sneakers all designed with Greek motifs. The most popular models are those sporting the Greek national flag. *Odós Dóna/Odós Ágion Pándon | Old Port*

### LALAÓUNIS (U E3) *(𝄞 e3)*

Greece's most renowned jeweller not only has branches in New York and on the Virgin Islands, but also in Corfu's Old Town. *Odós Kapodistríu 35 | on the northwest corner of the arcades on the Esplanade*

### VASSILÁKIS ★ ● 🌐
(U E2) *(𝄞 e2)*

Are you looking for a souvenir what you can find only on Corfu? Then look no further than the kumquat (or *koum kouat*), a citrus fruit grown exclusively on Corfu. This edible fruit closely resembling the orange is added to liqueur, ouzo and brandy, made into sweets and jams and its scent is even now used for perfumes. Nikos Vassilákis and his staff will let you try all the items on sale. *Daily 8am–midnight | Odós Spirídonos 61*

### VELVET
(U D3) *(𝄞 d3)*

Greek women's fashion designers are a rarity on Corfu. At least a few are on display here, in particular the labels Veloudákis and Zinás. *Odós N. Theotóki 42*

### WEEKLY MARKET ★ 🌐
(U B4) *(𝄞 b4)*

A real market with regional products! You won't find any souvenirs here, but things the locals need every day: fresh fish and pulses, nuts, fruit and vegetables, herbs and flowers. There are small cafés between the stands and the proprietors even take coffee to the dealers; lottery ticket sellers promise high winnings. *Mon–Sat 6am–2pm | in the moat beneath Odós Sp. Vlaikoj*

## SPORTS & BEACHES

Although you'll have to head out of town for sporting activities, you can enjoy a dip in the sea followed by a drink at the beach bar in Corfu Town. A more attractive destination is the lido at INSIDER TIP *Faliráki*, where the sun loungers are free for guests at the *Imabári* (see p. 46) beach bar. A more traditional address is the *Mon Repos Lido* (135 E6) (*D5*) )

style of Greek music; not sirtáki though, but metal, rock and the like. Those who prefer to stay in the Old Town should head up to the New Fort. There is a good nightlife scene around the fort's entrance. To kick off your evening, you can try the student pubs near the Old

Liqueurs in pretty bottles are not the only attraction at Vassilákis' in Kérkyra

at the southern end of the promenade. Both lidos offer fresh water showers and cubicles.

## ENTERTAINMENT

To the relief of locals, the island's party mile is located away from residential areas on the coastal road between the New Port and the city bypass. There is no regular bus service in the evenings but most partygoers take a taxi home. Except for a few stalwarts, the pubs and clubs along this mile change hands (and names) regularly though most offer ● free admission and the same

Port, the rooftop bar at the Hotel Cavalieri or the romantic seaside location of Faliráki.

### 54 DREAMY NIGHTS
(135 E5) (*D5*)

The hippest club (when we last checked...) on Corfu plays mainly deep house, hip-hop and Greek mainstream. The club's owners are particularly proud of their high-tech light shows and live music concerts. It usually attracts some of the town's VIPs who arrive in their sports cars rather than take a taxi home. *Leofóros Ethn. Antistáseos 54 | www.54drreamnights.com*

**INSIDER TIP ▶ GRAAL** (U B3) (*m b3*)

The alternative night spot playing jazz, jam and Latin swing and hosting the occasional live concert. The evening kicks off relatively early: from 10pm onwards crowds gather inside and outside directly under the walls of the New Fort. *Odós Solomoú 34 | www.facebook.com/graal. eraldicon*

**IMABÁRI** ★ (U F1) (*m f1*)

Chillaxe is the portmanteau to describe this seaside lounge bar named for no explicable reason after a Japanese town. The sun loungers become 'moon loungers' in the evening and if temperatures refuse to drop, you can cool down by dipping your feet into the sea. The designer cocktails are the best in town and the chef offers a small yet fine menu with creative Corfiot touches. *Daily from 9am | Faliráki Beach*

**INSIDER TIP ▶ POLYTÉCHNO**
(U B3) (*m b3*)

The hotspot for alternative party goers. The club specialises in experimental music and also hosts stand-up comedy nights, cartoon festivals and "koktéli naits" when rum takes centre stage. Get there by 9:30pm to gain entry. The program of events is posted on Facebook and on the board outside the club next to the entrance. *Odós Solomoú/Oddós Schoulemvoúrgou (New Fort) | tel. 26 61 02 77 94 | www.facebook.com/po lytechnocorfu*

**ROOF GARDEN CAVALIERI** ★ ☼
(U E5) (*m e5*)

A conservative venue offering bombastic views – the rooftop bar at the Hotel Cavalieri is a good location early evening, albeit its expensive prices. *Daily from 6pm | no admittance in shorts | Odós Kapodistríu 4*

**YARD CLUB**
(135 E5) (*m D5*)

This club specialises in theme nights. The best parties from Athens are repeated here on Wednesdays while the weekend brings "eKlectric Friday" and "Get so hot" on Saturdays with R'n'B. The Yard Club has been a stalwart on Corfu's clubbing scene for years. *Leofóros Ethn. Antistáseos 52 | www.facebook.com/Yard-Club*

## WHERE TO STAY

**BELLA VENEZIA**
(U D5) (*m d5*)

Atmospheric hotel in a Classicist building from the 19th century that was formerly a bank and then a school for girls. Each room is different and most have small balconies. Breakfast is served in the garden pavilion; the small bar opposite the lobby is the place to have an apéritif or nightcap in a relaxed environment. *32 rooms | Odós Zambelíu 4 | tel. 26 61 04 65 00 | www.bel laveneziahotel.com | Expensive*

**INSIDER TIP ▶ KONSTANTINOÚPOLIS**
(U C2) (*m c1*)

Are you looking for an adventure? Then check into the oldest hotel in town with its antiquated lift. In spite of its age, the lift has always been reliable over the years transporting a maximum of two people without luggage or one person with to the rooms above. You will also be woken up to the sound of the Greek national anthem coming from the nearby marine station when the Greek flag is hoisted. *34 rooms | Odós K. Zavitsianoú 11 | tel. 26 61 04 87 16 | booking via booking. com | Moderate*

### ACHÍLLION ★
(136 B2) (*D6*)

Emperors can be eccentric folk. The last Kaiser of Germany was certainly so. his family and red Mercedes car. The building of the castle was in fact commissioned by the Empress Elisabeth of Austria (1837–98), who visited her beloved Corfu from 1891 to her assassination in Geneva. She also loved this An-

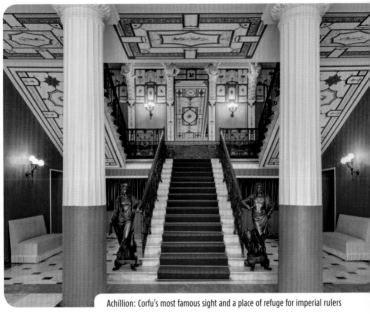

Achíllion: Corfu's most famous sight and a place of refuge for imperial rulers

Wilhelm II liked to sit on a stool shaped like a cavalry saddle – an oddity exhibited here as well as in the Netherlands where he was sent to exile. You are left wondering whether he signed the declaration to World War I while swaying to and fro on this rocking horse saddle. The Kaiser hero-worshipped the figure of the "victorious Achilles" and had a monument built in his memory with his helmet, shield and lance. The statue stands in the splendid gardens which the Kaiser bought along with the castle in 1907. Until the onset of World War I, he spent Easter here with cient Greek hero but, in keeping with her melancholic nature, chose to portray the "dying Achilles" in her garden statue. *May–Oct daily 8:30am–7pm; at other times Tue–Sun 8:45am–3:30pm | admission 7 euros*

You can taste the wines and liqueurs made by the *Vassilákis* distillery opposite Achíllion. *There are four to six buses daily to Achíllion – more in the high season – from San Rocco Square (line 10); tickets, also for the return trip, must be purchased in advance at the bus station or a kiosk; tickets are not available on the bus | 8 km (5 miles) from Kérkyra*

# THE NORTH

Although the whole of Corfu is beautiful, many believe the island's north to be the most stunning. If you hire a car for just one or two days, make sure you explore this region. The roads will take you on a roller coaster ride, winding up, down and around the massif formed by the island's highest peak, Pantokrátoras (906 m/3000 ft) and the steep bays along the coast.

Pretty little coves line the west coast below the coastal road which runs around the entire island. A 6 km (4 miles) long beach stretches along the north coast from Róda to beyond Acharávi. And in the west you can bathe on narrow strips of sand clinging to steep, rugged cliffs or the crescent-shaped bay of Ágios Geórgios. Venture through the ancient olive groves to discover old villages full of historic buildings that take you back in time – and a few ancient landmarks to complete the patchwork of landscape.

# ACHARÁVI & RÓDA

(134–135 C–D 1–2) (*ሠ C2*) **Are you looking for the ultimate beach holiday? Then the beach resorts of Acharávi (pop. 650) and Róda (pop. 370), which virtually merge together along the north coast, are a perfect choice of destination.** 6 km/3.7 miles long and 10–30 m/30–100 ft wide, this stretch of sand is virtually desolate in parts while crowded

## Long beaches and the highest mountain – the north is where Corfu shows its impressive variety best

with parasols and sun loungers in others. Beach bars conjugate around the centres and there is always a taverna in close vicinity. The resorts are packed with large all-inclusive hotels as well as affordable holiday flats and properties which attract a colourful mix of German and British holidaymakers. Over the years Corfiots have relocated to the inland villages and only visit the coast in summer. Olive groves stretch up behind the villages to the 900m/3000 ft Mount Pantokrátoras. Off the coast stand the Diapontia Islands

and the rocky Albanian mainland on the other side. You don't necessarily need to hire a car; a bike is a fun way to explore the region or buses run several times a day between both resorts and the island's capital as well as to the neighbouring villages of Kassiópi and Sidári. There is definitely enough to see and do on your beach holiday.

What differentiates the two resorts? Acharávi is the larger of the two yet its main shopping mile is located directly on the island's busy thoroughfare. Branch-

Pre-season – but even later there'll be enough room for everyone on the beach in Acharávi

ing off from this main road are dozens of small lanes leading down to the beach, none of which have street names but are numbered. There is no promenade as such and you need to wade through the sand to get from one beach bar to the next. In contrast Róda has a tiny centre along the seafront lined with restaurants and bars.

## SIGHTSEEING

There are no sights as such in the region as history has barely left its mark here. The resorts are not really idyllic, but only come to life in summer with the crowds of holidaymakers, who become an attraction in themselves, parading their tattooed and sunburnt bodies along the beach in tightly fitted bikinis and shorts. And then you should look at the ☀️ scenery around; the off-shore islands and mountains behind you are the spectacular sights.

## FOOD & DRINK

**INSIDER TIP** LEMON GARDEN

Even paradise has its flaws. Although lemons appear to be growing in every corner of the Lemon Garden restaurant, the fruits are too sour to eat. The trees however offer welcome shade in the hot summer heat. The owner Soúla never stops working from breakfast early morning to late into the night. A Greek folklore show is held twice a week where guests are taught traditional Greek dances and there is a Latin American night once a week. Meat and fish are grilled outside in the garden and under a traditional Corfiot wooden roof. The bar staff mix the best cocktails.

They make many of the products themselves: the strudel dough, limoncello and lemon marmalade. To resist the temptation of picking the lemons in this garden of paradise, take one for free from the baskets full of fruit (picked elsewhere!) at the exit. *Acharávi | on the main road 50 m/164 ft to the west of the roundabout | Moderate*

### PÁNGALOS

Tables on the terrace of the more than 180-year-old, repurposed warehouse are right on the shore. No other restaurant in Róda has a better location but the food is – like everywhere else in Róda – average at best. *Daily from 11am | Róda | on the coastal road in the village centre | Moderate*

### PUMPHOUSE

A real restaurant with real tablecloths, the glow of tea light candles, fresh flowers on the tables and easy-listening music in the background. Many dishes are served with tasty roast potatoes and the well-spiced *tas kebab*, a kind of stew with three types of meat, is outstanding. Large portions. *Daily from noon | Acharávi | at the roundabout | Expensive*

## SHOPPING

### OLIVE WOOD

"Grown to be a bike", was what the Corfu-born Polychrónis first thought on seeing a piece of olive wood and transformed it into a Harley Davidson. The life-size motorbike now hangs from the ceiling of his workshop along with a parrot who likes chatting to customers. As does Paulien, the wood carver's Dutch wife, who speaks several languages and explains how Polychrónis painstakingly makes household and decorative objects all made of olive wood. *On the road from the Dímitra supermarket to the beach, beach access no. 6 | Acharávi*

## SPORTS & BEACHES

The more than 6 km (3.7 miles) long beach of fine sand, with only a few pebbly patches, begins in Róda, makes its way past Acharávi and continues as *Almirós Beach* to the small island of *Agia Ekaterini* which can be reached over a footbridge. A 30-minute walk along a track will take you across the island to *Ágios Spirídonas* and, after another 15 minutes, you will reach the road around the island. You can then catch the bus back to Acharávi or Róda.

Guided two-hour tours on horseback are offered daily at 9am, 11am, 5pm and 7pm in Róda. The horses can be seen in a paddock on the road connecting the route around the island with the shore promenade. S-Bikes (see p. 112) offers

## MARCO POLO HIGHLIGHTS

★ **Paleó Períthia**
A village as it was in Venetian days and a rusti taverna far away from any road noise → p. 54

★ **Cape Drástis**
First the fairy-tale panorama and then a refreshing dip → p. 55

★ **Pantokrátor**
Corfu's highest mountain treats you to views out to Albania and the mainland opposite. → p. 54

★ **Kassiópi**
The island's most picturesque coastal resort → p. 58

★ **Afiónas**
Picture-perfect village with two beaches and fantastic tavernas → p. 56

★ **Angelókastro**
Romantic castle ruins high above a wild coastal scenery → p. 66

guided MTB tours almost daily and also hires mountain bikes. There are water sports facilities at the port in Róda and in front of the large hotels in Acharávi.

## ENTERTAINMENT

### HARRY'S BAR

"What's a bar without music?" says Harry. He also knows that a sports bar without the constant drone of football commentators in the background is not a sports bar. This explains the mixture of German and British voices, goal celebrations and the greatest hits from the Beatles and Rolling Stones coming from the bar's terrace filled with flowers and wide screens. Small droves of guests flock to this pub to enjoy the friendly service of Harry's daughter and Harry himself who is known for his authenticity and charm as well as for serving free shots to his guests. *Acharávi | at the east end of the old village road | www.harrysbar-apartments.com*

### YÁMAS

This is the place to go if you're looking for a late nightcap in Acharávi and Róda.

## LOW BUDGET

Live economically: the ten apartments at *Harry's Bar* in Acharávi (see above) are simple but spacious. *Tel. 26 63 06 30 38, mobile tel. 69 74 91 66 37 | studios from 15 euros | www.harrysbar-apartments.com*

A cheap swim: there are reduced prices in the *Hydropolis* fun pool (see p. 117) near Acharávi after 5pm. Adults only pay 11 euros and children (5–12 years) 7 euros.

But there is no guarantee that this pub will be open. *Acharávi, at the roundabout*

## WHERE TO STAY

### ACHARÁVI BEACH

Rows of expertly cut oleanders, lemon trees and palms decorate the garden of this hotel right at the beach. *97 rooms and apartments | Acharávi | east of the roundabout | tel. 26 63 06 31 02 | www.acharavibeach.com | Moderate*

### ST GEORGE'S BAY COUNTRY CLUB

This beach hotel is a perfect example of how best to adapt to the natural and historical surroundings. The 70 apartments, each accommodating up to four, are spread over a number of individually designed two-storey, island-style houses. Here, you almost feel that you are in a Corfiot village but with all mod cons and facilities. These include two flood-lit tennis courts, a clubhouse and restaurant, a spa area and large pool. *Acharávi | east of the roundabout | tel. 26 63 06 32 03 | www.stgeorgesbay.com | Expensive*

### TOURISTIC-ATELIER

Élena Vláchou's travel agency on the cul-de-sac leading to the Ionian Princess Hotel can arrange holiday apartments and houses in Acharávi. *Tel. 26 63 06 35 24*

## WHERE TO GO

### AGÍA EKATERÍNI
(135 D1) (*ⓜ C2*)

The northeast tip of Corfu is formed by the island of Agía Ekateríni that is covered by ferns and forests of pine, cypress and eucalyptus trees. There are no inhabitants here, even tavernas and beach bars are banned from the island. Bridges lead to the island; the one from Archarávi may only be used by pedestrians, cyclists and moped riders; the one to Ágios Spirídonas is also open to cars.

On the landside, it is enclosed by *Antoniótis,* a lake of brackish water that is rich in fish, and the two arms connecting it to the sea. The deserted *Agía Ekateríni* Monastery from 1713 lies hidden in a small forest. Paths also lead off of the main trail to small, almost deserted, shingle beaches where nude bathing is possible.

However, the 100-m/328 ft-long INSIDERTIP *sandy beach at Ágios Spirídonas* is much nicer; its gentle incline also makes it suitable for small children. There is a new, photogenic chapel right on the beach. *The Pyramid (www.corfu pyramid.com)* is located 200 m/656 ft away in the neighbouring bay with its stylish beach club, mini golf course, playground and beach restaurant. *8 km (5 miles) from Archarávi*

### ASTRAKÉRI
(134 C1) (*ØD B2*)

Are you wary of eating fish, squid and calamari? Then head to the taverna INSIDERTIP *Gregóris (signposted | Moderate)* to be converted. You will not find a more tenderly cooked or grilled octopus on the whole of Corfu. The calamari taste far different than the chewy rings of rubber available back home and the waiter will remove the bones before serving the freshly caught fish. Vassíli the owner usually waits on you in person and provides tips on how to best eat scampi if it's your first time. The traditional Corfiot *bourdétto* is on the daily menu to accompany dogfish shark or cuttlefish both served without bones. The langoustines are also affordable especially if Vassíli offers you Greek lobster, known as *kolopída* in Greek, meaning "langoust-

The Hydropolis is even more fun from 5pm when the admission costs less

ines without antennae". To enjoy the full range of specialities and atmosphere, we recommend staying for both lunch and evening meal and spend the time in between at the deserted sandy beach just 30 m/100 ft away. *6 km (3.7 miles) from Róda*

### NÍMFES
(134 C2) (*ØD C3*)

The INSIDERTIP *Naos Evstrámenou*, which is unique in the world and continues to baffle historians, is located on the outskirts of Nímfes. A dome similar to that of a Ceylonese dagoba – a form of Buddhist temple – rises up over a hexagonal base. Is the shape a coincidence or was the church designed by a Corfiot sailor after his journeys around the Indian Ocean? If you have always wanted to know how cumquats are grown, then head to the village centre where you can see the fruit growing in a large valley plantation below the village square. The church on your left probably dates from the 18th century. *Left of the road from Plátonas to Nímfes (signposted)*

### PALEÓ PERÍTHIA ★
### (135 E2) (*ØJ D3*)

Paleó Períthia looks like a museum village from the Venetian period. Situated in a fertile, high-altitude valley below Pantokrátor, it was quite well-off in former days as can be seen by the large, sturdy stone houses and churches. However, its inhabitants moved down to the coast where they founded *Néa Períthia* (New Períthia). Only a few elderly shepherds remained. The village fell into oblivion

and escaped the cementing boom of the 1970s and 80s.

In the early 1990s, the first tavern opened and, today, there are four. The locals like the *Taverna Fóros* best – also INSIDER TIP because of its excellent walnut cake. another tip: Ask the owner Thomas for a business card, he will draw you one in a matter of seconds! *Buses only twice a day to Loútses, then 3 km (1.9 mile) on foot | 15 km (9.3 miles) from Archarávi*

### PANTOKRÁTOR ★ ⋙
### (135 E2–3) (*ØJ D3*)

Once you have reached the top you can't get any higher on the island. At an altitude of 906 m/3000 ft, the view from the summit is breath-taking encompassing the whole island and, on clear days, reaches as far as Albania and the Greek mainland. But don't be deceived: what often appears to be the boot of Italy in the distance is just a layer of mist! A tarmac road takes you up the moun-

Cape Drástis – the steep cliffs in the northwest can only be reached on foot or by boat

tain to the narrow car park on the mountain ridge where it can be a hair-raising experience trying to turn your vehicle. Walk past a small café to reach the aptly-named monastery Pantokrátoras which literally translates as the "Almighty", clearly a reference to Jesus Christ rather than the mountain itself. Since 1998, it has been occupied once again in the summer months – alternately by a priest from a nearby mountain village and a monk from a Corfiot monastery. Since then, time-consuming restoration of the church frescoes has taken place and some of them have now regained their 17th century splendour. The monastery is open every day to visitors. *26 km (16 miles) from Nissáki*

## PERULÁDES ᠅
(134 A2) *(𝄞 A2)*

Have no fear; the skywalk at Peruládes (pop. 780) is strong enough to bear many a tourist. You will be treated to

thrilling views of the narrow sandy beach stretching below the cliffs. Steps lead down to the beach from the car park in front of the open-air bar *Panórama/7th Heaven (daily | Moderate–Expensive)* Charging relatively expensive prices, the bar offers seating on its spacious lawn or at tables directly on the cliff's edge. The restaurant, *7th Heaven (daily | Expensive)*, serves, if not heavenly, then good food next door.

Make sure to visit the ★ ᠅ *Cape Drástis* beforehand! Of all of Corfu's beautiful coastal landscapes, this one at the far northwest tip of the island is the nicest. Below the almost 100 m/328 ft high snowy-white cape, sandstone formations like dragons' combs surround a small bay with a little rocky island that looks like a shark's fin in front of it. The path begins at the clearly recognisable primary school along the village road. There is initially a slight incline after which it runs down to the sea and then, all of a sudden, you have the picture-book panorama of the bay in front of you. You can continue following the track by car, jeep, and bike or on foot until it ends in a tiny bay surrounded by rocks. If the sea is calm, you can jump into the water here and enjoy a swim in the crystal-clear sea with a view of the steep, light-coloured cliffs that tower up right out of the water. *16 km (10 miles) from Acharáv*

## SIDÁRI
(134 B1–2) *(𝄞 B 2)*

Sidári (pop. 400) is like a fairground. There is a string of bars, travel agencies and souvenir shops along the main street; nothing is left of its former charm. The lingua franca is Greek only in winter; in summer, everyone speaks English. The pools are flooded with rock music and there is hardly a bar that doesn't have a large screen for sporting events.

If it wasn't for the heat, you could be forgiven for thinking you are back in the UK.

But there is a different, more picturesque side to Sidári at the coves along the 🌿 Canal d'Amour where several low-lying rocky headlands project out to sea, some with caves below. The narrow strips of sand are no way large enough to accommodate the crowds of sun-worshippers who come here. Sun loungers spread out across the green hills, cliff terraces and the lawns in front of hotels and tavernas. For a spot of fun and action, hire a pedal boat or swim out to the off-shore rocky outcrops. You won't be alone here but the views are unique. *8 km (5 miles) from Róda*

### STRINÍLAS 🌿 (135 D2–3) (*M C3*)

Do you have a head for heights? Then take a trip which combines the highest mountain and the highest village on the island. Drive up the Pantokrátoras followed by a break at the *Taverna Oasis (daily | Budget)* on the tiny *platía* of this mountain village. The 200-year old elm under which you are now sitting is also the oldest on the island. *10 km (6.2 miles) from Acharávi*

# ÁGIOS GEÓR-GIOS & CO.

(134 A–B 2–3) (*M A3*) **Four resorts all beginning with A and all guaranteeing a great holiday: Ágios Geórgios North, Arillás, Ágios Stéfanos are straddled along the coast while the inland village ⭐ Afiónas towers above the other three perched on the mountain ridge.**

All three coastal resorts are a haven for sun worshippers with their long stretches of sandy beaches. Although they have managed to ward off large hotel complexes and all-inclusive accommodation, the resorts are still vibrant places with a good selection of bars and tavernas. The village of Afiónas offers an idyllic rural backdrop with its excellent tavernas and delightful setting. From there you can walk down to the beach of *Pórto Timióni* situated around two separate coves. This bay is not accessible by car or moped.

## FOOD & DRINK

### EVDAÍMON 🌿 🌐

You will not be disappointed with the standard of cooking in this restaurant. Jánnis from Corfu and Evangelía from Athens conjure up a new menu every day, using only the finest and freshest ingredients. The flat-pea puree *fava*, originating from the island of Santorini, replaces the common-place tzatziki which is now even available in supermarkets back home. All the sauces and dishes are homemade with a generous addition of herbs. This splendid cuisine is accompanied by amazing views especially at sunset. *Daily from 1pm | Afiónas | on the main road | Moderate*

## SHOPPING

### CORFU BREWERY 🌐

A toast to Corfu and this, still the only brewery on the island! This is a young venture in need of support. Guided tours are organised on Saturdays and its shop is open six days a week selling eight different types of brews, beer glasses, etc. *Mon–Sat 9am–3pm, guided tours only Sat 10:30am–12:30pm | Arillás | next to the service station on the road to Magouládes*

Whoever swims through the Canal d'Amour will fall in love – as the old legend goes

## ÍLIOS LIVING ART ●

The perfect place for the romantically minded and shell collectors. The jewellery designer Alex can cast miniature olive pits, things you have found or that have been washed up on the shore, in bronze, silver or gold for you to wear as a pendant in less than 40 minutes. *Ágios Geórgios Pagón | on the road to the beach | www.ilios-living-art.com*

**INSIDER TIP** ▶ OLIVES AND MORE ◒

This is where you can find first-class olive oil and products made of it, as well as creations conjured up by the owners Heidi and Rainer themselves. They produce olive paste, preserve olives and fill olive oil into tins you can take with you on the plane. If you like, you can even get it straight from the barrel. Heidi also teaches acrylic painting in four-hour-courses. *Sun–Fri 10am–2pm and 3–9pm, Sat only 3–9pm | Afíonas | at the top end of the village square*

## BEACHES

You can decide for yourself how much (or how little) you want to wear on the 2 km (1.2 mile) long beach between Aríllás and Ágios Stéfanos as long as you keep a discrete distance away from the resort's centre. Water sports enthusiasts should head to *Sun & Fun Watersports (tel. 69 74 31 71 99 | www.sunfunclubcorfu.blogspot.com)* on the Ágios Geórgios beach in front of Hotel Alkyon. They have jet bikes, water skis, canoes, paddle and motor boats for hire. You can also take a taxi-boat to Timióni Beach which can otherwise only be reached on foot..

## ENTERTAINMENT

The resort has many bars; none in particular are worth mentioning. Go where the party takes you or start one yourself, for example at *Ámmos* in Aríllás, *Bar 38* in Ágios Stéfanos or *Dichtiá* in Ágios Geórgios.

# KASSIÓPI

**INSIDER TIP** HONIGTAL

Nestled between old olive groves, this delightful accommodation in the sweet-sounding "honey valley" houses five small apartments and its owners are intent on making their guests feel extremely welcome during their stay. Situated just 500m/1600ft from the beach, the farm invites families as well as groups of friends to enjoy the rural landscape around. Children will make friends easily on the donkey or pony rides or on the farm's large playground while adults get to know each other on the mountain bike tours and hikes. Everyone can take part in the farm workshops organised by the head manager Marios where you can help cleaning the stables or picking tomatoes. Prices include bed, breakfast and evening meal with food served in the farm's own restaurant which caters for vegetarians and vegans and offers a varied and wholesome breakfast. Visit their homepage to learn more about the eleven members of staff. *Ágios Geórgios Págon | tel. 26 63 09 63 48 | www.honigtalaufkorfu.de | Moderate*

**INSIDER TIP** PANORAMA

Enjoy the last glass of wine before bed and the first cup of coffee in the morning accompanied by the beguiling views from the balconies and terraces from the four apartments. The house is reached down a few steps from the restaurant with a small car park above. Leave the village behind and you will almost feel like a captain on board an ocean liner enjoying your own private views of the sea, beaches, cliffs and islands around. *Afiónas | on the main street | tel. 26 63 0518 46 | www.panoramacorfu.com | Budget*

(135 E1–2) *(⑭ D2)* ★ **Kassiópi is not one of your usual beachside resorts. This coastal village has its own population of 1100 inhabitants who live there all year round. You almost get the feeling that they could survive pretty well without us tourists.**

From the village there is no beach or large hotel in sight. Instead you are treated to a picturesque harbour and narrow lanes bursting with tavernas and bars as well as an authentic *kafenío* and even a tiny *platía* with everything there, from a bus stop to post office. On closer look, you'll discover the remains of the Venetian fortress walls towering up between the trees above the harbour buildings – and the rectory on the roof of the village church. Now you're probably curious. Take your time to explore this little gem.

### SIGHTSEEING

#### CASTLE (KASTRO)

Over the past few years, the EU has invested millions in the castle that the Venetians built in 1386 on top of the remains of an old fortress. The interior, completely overgrown by scrub, is illuminated at night (but why? one might wonder, since there's only chicken and sheep there) and a sprinkler system ensures its protection from fire. The gatehouse has been restored and improvements made to the outer walls with their 13 towers. Whether this is the right kind of financial aid Greece needs is debatable. *Free access | the path to the castle begins on the main road to the harbour opposite Panagía Kassiópitra Church*

### PANAGÍA KASSIÓPITRA CHURCH

Today priests are spared the task of climbing onto the roof to enter the rectory which is still visible on top of the St Mary's church today. Although the rectory is closed to the public, the church is open every day. It was built in 1590 on the site of an ancient Roman temple frequented by the likes of the mad Emperor Nero and Cicero. Rumour has it that even Cleopatra also set foot in the temple. That's because in ancient Greek and medieval times, Kassiópi was a popular stop-off for ships sailing between Greece and Italy. After a stormy crossing from the boot of Italy, travellers could recuperate here from a bout of seasickness or wait until the waters were calmer to attempt the return journey. *Access from the main road to the harbour and the terrace of the The Old School tavern at the harbour*

### FOOD & DRINK

### JÁNIS

The white-blossoming yucca palms in late summer are alone worth the visit to one of the resort's largest tavernas. Although primarily catering for its British guests, the dishes try to show the tourists the idea of authentic Greek food. This is why the taverna also offers a Corfiot-style *mezedákia* with lots of small portions of fresh food brought to the table. You are encouraged to try different tastes away from the typical tourist dishes. *Daily | where the one-way road from the harbour meets the circular island road | Expensive*

A great place for relaxing and eating: the seafront restaurants at Kassiópi

### TAVERNÁKI

Searching for the perfect location for a romantic occasion? Then look no further than this delightful taverna. Designed in natural stone and wood, the building is decorated with flowers and candlelight to set the romantic mood. Besides the usual tourist menu, the restaurant also serves more creative dishes such as dried cod fish cakes. It is advisable to book a table due to the restaurant's popularity. *Daily | easterns ide of the harbour basin | tel. 26 63 08 15 29 | Moderate*

## SPORTS & BEACHES

5 minutes on foot from the north end of the harbour is the 80 m/260 ft long *Batería Beach* on the peninsula crowned with the castle. Deckchairs and umbrellas are available to hire on the coarse sandy beach as well as under the olive trees around the bay. From the south end of the harbour, a small path leads you to a few rocky outcrops where you can also sunbathe. The 200 m/650 ft coarse sandy *Main Beach* skirts Kassiópi's north-western bay near the Yánis taverna. The most beautiful beach is the *Avláki Beach* (a pebbly beach 500 m/1640 ft long) to the south which takes 30 minutes to reach on foot from Kassiópi.

At the *Avláki Beach* the *Corfu Sailing Centre (tel. 69 34 30 50 47 | www.corfu sailingcentre.com)* specialises in windsurfing and sailing courses but also has equipment, SUP boards and kayaks for hire. Corfu's first motor boat rental agency fills the harbour of Kassiópi with its

Batería Beach in Kassiopi may be narrow, but it boasts a beautiful location

motor boats. Those without a boat licence have to settle with a 30 HP boat to ride the waves. Boats are available from *Filíppos Rent-a-boat (tel. 26 63 08 12 27 | www.filippos-boats.com)* and kayaks and paddle boats can also be hired on Batería Beach. Scuba diving courses are organised by *Corfu Divers (on the main road | tel. 26 63 02 92 26 | www.corfu-divers.com)* If you prefer horses to seahorses, contact *Dímitris Katsáros (on the road from Avláki Beach to Ágios Stéfanos | www.dimitriscorfu.gr)* who arranges guided tours on horseback.

## ENTERTAINMENT

There are no discos or clubs in Kassiópi. Evenings are spent at the seafront bars, on the *platía* or at *Kóstas Bar* on the road between the harbour and village square where Greek dancing is held every evening starting from 10pm.

## WHERE TO STAY

### BELLA MARE

Situated 2 km/1.2 mile from Kassiópi, you can "seriously relax" at this apartment-hotel at Avláki Beach. Studios and apartments are divided between the three two-storey buildings in traditional Corfu architecture which are nestled between large lawns and a pool.
The 500 m/1640 ft pebbly beach has just two tavernas. A water sports station and riding stables are in close vicinity. It's worth hiring a car if you don't want to spend all your time at the beach. *21 rooms | tel. 26 63 08 19 97 | www.belmare.gr | Moderate–Expensive*

### MELÍNA BAY

The Italian architect Alberto Artuso moved to Corfu in 2005 and specialises in set and light design. He designed the rooms and lighting of this tiny boutique hotel situated directly on the Kassiópi harbour. All balconies face the port; the bar and restaurant are also part of the harbour promenade. *22 rooms | tel. 26 63 08 10 30 | www.melinabay.com | Moderate*

### ROOMS ARAKINOÚ

A popular haunt for backpackers and hippy travellers way back in the 1960s, this old-fashioned guesthouse accommodates four basic rooms around a small courtyard above a row of seafront shops. Although this B&B is not known for its comfort factor, the owner Helena takes good care of her guests who get to know each other easily in the courtyard. Who knows – maybe your grandma and grandpa became an item here... *On the main road opposite the entrance to the churchyard | tel. 26 63 08 12 31 | Budget*

## WHERE TO GO

### ÁGIOS STÉFANOS SINIÉS
### (135 F2) (∅ E3)

Ágios Stéfanos Siniés (pop. 230) is the closest Corfiot village to Albania which may or may not be reason enough to drive down to this tiny village. If not, maybe one of the island's best fish restaurants can entice you? Some of the tables and chairs of the *Eucalyptus (daily | Moderate–Expensive)* are positioned directly on the beach. You choose your fish from the glass counter and the waiters are experts in the art of removing the bones before serving it. The neighbouring tables are normally occupied by sailors who have anchored their yachts in the secluded bay. *6 km (3.7 miles) from Kassiópi*

### AGNÍ
(135 F2) *(M D3)*

Agní is a small, peaceful bay with a 150 m/492 ft-long, white shingle-and-stone beach, a few private rooms and three tavernas. Wooden jetties where yachts moor jut out into the water. The three inns all serve good fresh fish. There are many dishes for vegetarians on the menu of the *Agní* tavern *(daily | Budget)* – *marída jemistá*, sardines filled with cheese, garlic and parsley, are quite innovative. Scampi pilaf, *piláfi me gárides*, is the hit in *Toula's Taverna (daily | Budget)*. You should use the car park on the outskirts of the village; it is often impossible to turn at the waterside! *11 km (6.8 miles) from Kassiópi*

### KALÁMI
(135 F3) *(M E3)*

The tiny hamlet of Kalámi on the coast is almost smothered by a large holiday club complex. A visit can be recommended for fans of Lawrence Durrell's Corfu classic "Prospero's Cell". The Durrell family lived in Kalámi in the 1930s – in the large property on the shore called *White House (tel. 26 63 09 10 40 | www.white-house-corfu.gr | Budget)*. The four-bedroomed building can be rented as a holiday house; the Durrell family's dining table is still there! There is now a good taverna on the ground floor *(daily | Budget)*.

The 250 m/820 ft-long pebble-and-stone beach is relatively small for so many summer holidaymakers. However, there is a track from here to *Gialiskári Beach* in the north where there are a lot less people on the pebbly beach and rocks. This is also an interesting underwater world for snorkelers. *11 km (6.8 miles) from Kassiópi*

### KAMINÁKI BEACH
(135 E3) *(M D3)*

The much-photographed shingle beach, measuring just 100 × 15 m/328 x 49 ft, lies in front of a tiny coastal settlement with two tavernas *(Budget)* and a water sports business *(www.kaminakiboats.com)* that also rents out motorboats without a skipper. There are around 60 loungers under 30 sunshades on the beach, but there is always enough space for your towel if you prefer.

### KULÚRA (135 F3) *(M E3)*

The semi-oval harbour basin in front of the fortified country seat from the 16th century in Kulúra is one of Corfu's standard postcard images. It is worth taking a photo but a waste of time driving down to the harbour where there are hardly any parking spaces. The house has belonged to an Italian family since 1986 and is off-limits to holidaymakers. *10 km (6.2 miles) from Kassiópi*

Paleokastrítsa and the adjoining coastal areas are among the most beautiful on Corfu

# PALEO-KASTRÍTSA

**(134 B4)** *(⌀ B4)* **) When Corfiots are asked to name the most beautiful place on Corfu, most answer with Paleokastrítsa. In short, it is a place of superlatives and explains why most cruise ship passengers head straight to the village after descending from their off shore luxury liners. They are content with admiring the view from their ship, from the water and from the cliffs above.**

When you arrive in Paleokastrítsa, you are more likely left wondering where the actual centre is. The road stretches 3 km/1.8 mile from the village entrance sign to the seafront where it comes to an end. Except for a handful of hotel and shops and a few signs pointing to village tavernas, this appears to be it. There is no centre as such and there has never been one; the blanket of olive groves has always covered the sprinkling of houses and the small bays for bathing as well as the port are also hidden from sight. Even the village's most famous attraction, its monastery, cannot be spotted from the village. The best way of exploring the true charm of Paleokastrítsa and its surrounding landscape is to take a boat ride or drive up to the mountain village of Lákones.

## SIGHTSEEING

### BOAT TOUR

The whole day long skippers stand waiting for visitors to arrive where the road ends at the large car park and the village's only traffic lights. They take guests on a 40-minute boat ride along the bay of Paleokastrítsa, which – to be precise – consists of many tiny coves. They sail up close to the sea coves and caves and beaches which can only be reached by boat along the precipitous, green coastline and rugged cliffs on which the village's most famous monastery stands. It is an active beach getaway perfect for outdoor enthusiasts who most often hire a boat on their own and head to the many solitary beaches.

### PANAGÍA THEOTÓKU TIS PALEOKASTRÍTSAS MONASTERY ★

It's ironic that almost nobody enters a monastery today yet crowds of people flock to visit this one every summer. To capture a halfway decent picture of the monastery's impressive location, walk past the monastery taverna and cemetery for 5 minutes along the seafront. You will notice that the white monastery perches on a precipitous headland in front of steep cliffs.

With its shady arcades, elegant arches, courtyard full of flowers and discrete 18th century buildings, the *Panagía Theotókou tis Paleokastrítsas* (monastery of "The Holy Bearer of God of Paleokastrítsa") is an idyllic location. The perfect photo of the monastery is complete if you manage to catch a shot of one of the three monks who still live there.

The paintings inside the church remind of a time without photography when events had to be captured by artists. The church's most precious icon has been placed at the front on the left-hand wall. The work from 1653 only measures 43 × 33 cm and shows three Fathers of the Church identifiable by their stoles decorated with crosses. Behind them, there is a depiction of a dramatic event that actually occurred

Tourist magnet: the romantic monastery Panágia Theotóku tis Paleokastrítsas

in Corfu on the feast day of these three saints, on 30 January, in 1653. A firework that had been lit in their honour exploded while a nurse holding a child in her arms was standing nearby. As if by miracle, the child remained uninjured although the nurse was killed. She can be seen clearly in the right-hand section of the painting. Blood is pouring out of her side, she falls to the ground while still holding the child in her arms. The child's parents donated the icon as a sign of their gratitude to the saints for this (modest) miracle; the text to the right of the strip of pictures gives a detailed description of the occurrence.

There are two other icons at the back of the church on the left-hand and right-hand walls. They were painted in 1713 and illustrate four scenes of the Creation. The illustrations of animals are both cute and naïve. *April–Oct daily 7am–1pm and 3–8pm; the best time to visit is before 9am and after 5pm when the hordes of tourists have left the church. Whatever you do, don't park in the spaces reserved for buses – the drivers will block you in mercilessly! | admission free*

## FOOD & DRINK

### HORIZON ⤴

The splendid location of this taverna is hidden away from sight, as is so typical for Paleokastrítsa. Only by following the steps leading down from the road will you be treated to panoramic views of the magnificent bay. Great service, good food. *Daily | on the main road, next to Hotel Odysseus | Paleokastrítsa | Moderate*

## SHOPPING

### STREET MARKET

A row breaks out in the village every year between street dealers who want to set up their stands as close to the monastery as possible to attract the buses full of tourists. And the local council who would prefer to move them along to the drab car park at the traffic lights, hidden away from the cruise passengers. It's worth a look around just to see who has the upper hand in this dispute! Africans sell arts and crafts from their native countries and Corfiots 🌐 natural products and painted objects of all sorts. The pebbles painted with Corfiot motifs make nice little gifts or look good on your window sill at home.

## BEACHES

The pebble beaches in the three large bays *Ambeláki*, *Spíridon* and *Alípa* are easy to reach. Flights of steps lead from the main road down to other smaller pebbly bays. *Liapádes'* shingle beach is around 150 m/492 ft long. None of them are really ideal for children. Boat taxis leave from *Spíridon Beach*, the pier in front of the La Grotta Bar, the harbour at *Alípa Beach* and *Liapádes Beach* for the numerous other ● sandy and shingle bays that can only be reached from the sea.

## ENTERTAINMENT

### INSIDER TIP ▸ LA GROTTA

For a spectacular setting and a heavy dose of kitsch, take the 142 steps leading down to the seafront, leaving reality behind you to enter a fantasy world with an artificial cave, rock faces lit up in colour, straw parasols and wooden walkways over the water. The night owls are in fact bats and you can even spot fish diving out of the water. The sounds of the waves are accompanied by the soft background music. The ultimate place to chill out and maybe go for a night swim. *Daily | Paleokastrítsa*

## WHERE TO STAY

### AKROTIRI BEACH ☼☼
Do it in style. This classic 1970s hotel overlooks the sea from its cliff side location. It boasts a large cliff terrace pool and a smaller pool next to the *Beach Taverna* on the fine sandy beach. There is a lift which takes you down to the beach and all rooms have balconies overlooking the bay. Jazz evenings are held in the *Akron Bar*. The hotel provides free mountain bikes and water sport facilities at a cost. And if you want a change of scenery, there is a bus stop just 30m/100ft away from the hotel where you can catch a bus to the island's capital. *126 rooms | on the main road | tel. 26 63 04 12 75 | www.akotriri-beach.com | Expensive*

### INSIDER TIP ► VILLA FIORITA STUDIOS
Hotels are not your thing? Then try this guesthouse run by the very friendly Loúlis family situated halfway along the main road. The bougainvillea-covered balconies and blue and white shutters give the guesthouse its traditional Hellenic feel. The next beach is just 150m/500ft away. *15 studios | main road | Paleokastrítsa | tel. 26 63 04 13 52 | www.villa-fiorita. paleokastritsa.hotels-corfu.com | Moderate*

## WHERE TO GO

### ANGELÓKASTRO ★ ☼☼
(134 B4) (*ØØ B4*)
A race to the top! You can reach the castle from the car park in just five minutes, but most take 10 minutes at a gentler pace. Whatever your speed, the views from the top will stop you in your tracks: The ruins of this Byzantine-Venetian "Angels' Castle" are a fascinating sight. They stand high above the west coast on a mountain peak with steep slopes on all sides. The panorama is just as breathtaking as the walk up. Until the last Turkish invasion of the island in 1716, this repeatedly offered refuge to the population of northern Corfu when enemies or pirates approached. Nobody was ever able to conquer Angelókastro. A tarmac road leads from Makrádes to a car park 700 m/2,296 ft beyond Kriní at the foot of the castle hill with a small taverna *(Budget)*. You'll have to walk up a steep path for the last 7 to 10 minutes but you will be rewarded with a wonderful view for your effort. *Freely accessible out of season, in the summer daily 8am–7pm, admission 2 euros | 10 km (6.2 miles) from Paleokastrítsa*

### LÁKONES ☼☼ (134 B4) (*ØØ B4*)
The whole of Lákones is one large balcony. The village survives from its amazing view over Paleokastrítsa including its monastery and bays, steep coastline and green hills all around. Those who had or could borrow money, built cafés and tavernas here commanding panoramic views; the main reason why people come here. Visit *Castellino (Expensive)*, the region's highest restaurant to try their homemade walnut cake or *Café Dolce (Budget)*, which serves an espresso you'd expect only in Italy. If you are looking for a wild time, join in the all-day parties of tour groups – mainly from Eastern Europe – around the pool at the *Golden Fox (Moderate)*. which always welcome new faces. All the pubs and restaurants are well-signposted from the village road. *5 km/3.1 miles from Paleokastrítsa*

## MAKRÁDES
### (134 B4) (*Ⓜ B4*)

Makrádes (pop. 300) appears as a place from another time with its century-old houses and narrow lanes where no car dares to go. Nowhere else on Corfu have so many inhabitants specialised in selling herbs and local table wine as here. Fierce competition forces them to make furious attempts to stop any passing car! In the Colombo Taverna *(daily | Budget)* on the village square there is a more than 200-year-old olive press and you can sample many Corfiot specialities and all kinds of meat from the charcoal grill. Situated in the middle of the countryside on the edge of the village is the well-signposted café INSIDER TIP *Spíti Tichí (Sun/Mon, Wed/Thu 10am–5pm | Budget)*, where you can try their excellent breakfasts and even tastier cakes served underneath the fig, mulberry and orange trees with fantastic views over the landscape around. The landlady offers tips on short hikes in the local area. *9 km (5.6 miles) from Paleokastrítsa*

Perfectly built on the top of a cliff: Angelókastro Castle

# THE SOUTH

Certainly less spectacular than the island's dramatic north, Corfu's south still has its own special charm with a lake, two photogenic river harbours, a magical forest and miles of sandy beaches with dunes and steep cliffs. Glow worms can be spotted in summer and pink flamingos are a special treat for tourists who arrive early on or very late in the year. The roads are far less winding than in the north and you feel less rushed to cram in all the sights.

The majority of the large hotels run by travel operators line the coast between Benítses and Messongí with one in Ágios Górdis and one near Lefkími. Most other tourists stay in small guesthouses and apartments with the evening's enter-tainment provided by a handful of taver-nas and bars. The advantage (or maybe disadvantage) is you are guaranteed to bump into someone you met the night before.

# ÁGIOS GEÓRGIOS SOUTH

(136 C5) (*ⁿ D–E8*) **Some beaches just resemble one large sand pit. But not in ★ Ágios Geórgios South.**

A miniature desert-like dune landscape starts where all roads end directly on the northern edge of the resort. The

Corfu's gentler side: olive groves, beaches that are easy to reach, Lake Koríssion and many peaceful coastal towns

dunes stretch as far as Corfu's largest inland lake from where a narrow 5 km/3 mile-long spit spreads out between brackish water and sea water, separated from the sea by a narrow, and in parts wider, strip of sand with pebbles. This is a tranquil spot for anyone seeking peace and quiet. For the more adventurous, a surf, SUP and kite station is situated at the northern end of the spit. Those looking for a little evening entertainment should head to Ágios Geórgios along its 2 km/1.2 mile long promenade

which also offers a long stretch of beach starting in the south.

## SIGHTSEEING

### LAKE KORÍSSION
(136 B–C 4–5) (*M D7–8*)

Fins would be less impressed for they have thousands, but the Corfiots are very proud of their Lake Koríssion, namely the only inland lake on the island. The lake is 5 km (3.1 miles) long and up to 1000 m/3281 ft wide and is separated

Only a small strip of land separates Lake Koríssion from the sea

from the sea by a strip of sand and dunes but connected to it by a narrow, natural channel. The sea virtually splits in half the spit between Ágios Geórgios in the south and the tiny village of Chalikoúnas in the north. This narrow channel is crossed by a footbridge and if you walk past the water sports station to the other end, you will reach the small sandy bay at Alonáki, home to one of the island's best tavernas. Both the taverna and water sports station can be reached by car, although the way is not that easy to find.

## FOOD & DRINK

### ALONÁKI ★ ●

You will feel like you are in the Garden of Eden when you sit in this idyllic taverna above the small bay with its sandy beach to the north of the long dune beach at Chalikúnas. A myna bird chatters and laughs in its aviary, cats vie for your attention and swallows nest under the wooden roof of the terrace. Apricots and figs fall almost directly into your mouth. The innkeeper's family serves delicacies including rabbit *stifádo*, *skórpios bourdéto* and stuffed cabbage leaves – *lachanodolmádes*. *Daily | well signposted from the road to Chalikúnas beach | Budget*

### INSIDER TIP ● O KAFÉSAS ✂

In the most unusual taverna in Ágios Geórgios, you sit on terraces above a little-used road with a view of the sea. Ákis the proprietor has decorated the taverna tastefully. The bread comes straight out of the clay oven; the vegetables, olive oil and chickens are from his farm and the fish is home-smoked. The mixed pickles – *toursí* – are in a league of their own and the *bourdétto* is made with stingray. There is usually live Greek music on Saturday evenings. *Daily | on the coast road in the south of the village | Moderate*

## SPORTS

Ágios Geórgios South is the best place for windsurfing and the only resort on the island to offer kite surfing. The latest

out to the sounds of music and splashing waves. During the day it caters mainly for mountain bikers and surfers who also gather there in the evenings for a chat. *Daily | at the northern end of the coastal road*

## WHERE TO STAY

### INSIDER TIP ALONÁKI

This guesthouse offers an alternative type of accommodation in simply furnished rooms with and without kitchen facilities (40 and 35 euros respectively) and far away from any other hotel. Corfiot food is served in the guesthouse's garden taverna. There is a tiny sandy beach right in front of the house. Another

trend is stand-up paddling and guided tours are organised by *Kite Club Corfu (tel. 69 77 14 56 14 | www.kite-club-corfu.com)* at Chalikoúnas Beach to the north of the spit; for more information on all these activities, go to the *Harley* café at the northern end of the promenade.

## ENTERTAINMENT

**HARLEY**

This cafe is open all day and develops into a lively meeting place for surfers in the evening. This is where they not only talk shop and listen to good music but also play *távli* and *KoJa golf* – a natural kind of miniature golf developed by the owners, Bavaria-born Anita and her Greek husband Jánnis. *Daily | At the northern end of the coastal road*

**MANGO BAR** ☼

The crowd makes all the difference and non-club members are invited to join in the party at this sports club from 9pm onwards. The relaxing colours of the walls, sofas and cocktails invite guests to chill-

### ★ Alonáki
Good food in a wonderful garden setting in Chalikúnas
→ p. 70

### ★ Lefkími
Corfu's prettiest river port – photogenic but not (yet) overcrowded → p. 72

### ★ Paramónas
A peaceful beach resort with small hotels and good tavernas → p. 75

### ★ Ágios Geórgios South
Sand and dunes like nowhere else on the island → p. 68

### ★ Chlómos
An impressive mountain village of tiled-roofed buildings with magnificent panoramic views → p. 78

**MARCO POLO HIGHLIGHTS**

unspoilt beach is situated just ten minutes away with just two beach bars and one water sports station, that's it. It is the perfect place to switch off and unwind away from any distractions; there is no bus stop in front of the door and no disco far and wide. The owner Katarína warmly welcomes guests and the rest of the family speak good English if you would like to book in advance by phone. *Tel. 26 61 07 58 72 | www.facebook.com/ alonaki-bay | Budget*

### GOLDEN SANDS

Admittedly, your grandad and grandma would feel at home here yet this two-storey hotel still attracts a mixed crowd of guests. Situated directly on the promenade just 100m/330ft from the next beach, the hotel offers a laid-back atmosphere, pool and large balconies. Travellers on a round trip of the island can park up here and get a decent room for just one night. *78 rooms | southern part of town | tel. 26 62 05 12 25 | www.corfugolden sands.com | Budget*

## WHERE TO GO

### GARDÍKI
(136 B4) (*Ø D 7*)

The 13th-century Byzantine castle, with its octagonal defence wall and towers of quarried stone with rows of brick, is the most important historical site in the southern part of the island. Due to danger of collapse, going inside is strictly forbidden. *13 km (8.1 miles) from Ágios Geórgios*

### KÁVOS
(137 F6) (*Ø G8*)

The island's most southerly resort is the place to party (especially for British and Irish tourists) on Corfu (pop. 850). The beach is narrow and overrun with young people while the main street is more crowded at 4 in the morning than in the afternoon. By sunrise, the street is covered in broken bottles and drunken teenagers trying to find their way back to their hotel. What else can you expect when the shots are handed out for less than a euro? *22 km (13.7 miles) from Ágios Geórgios | English website: www.ka vosnightlife.com*

### LEFKÍMI ★
(137 E5) (*Ø F8*)

Despite being the largest town in the south (pop. 3500), Lefkími has remained almost untouched by tourism. Accommodation is scarce and there is only a handful of tavernas and one popular café along the riverbank running on both sides of the bridge. One kilometre away from the town, the River Chimarós flows into the sea next to a beautiful sandy beach, which has only one snack

bar and no water activities to offer.
The river was once the town's *port* housing small warehouses and workshops; today it is the town's most photogenic attraction. Provided you have a good zoom function on your camera, another sight worth capturing is the INSIDER TIP hundreds of pink flamingos which flock to the former saltworks at *Alikés* every year between October and May. The shore here is extremely flat and suitable even for small children. The only taverna along the shore rents out a handful of parasols and sun loungers. *16 km (9.9 miles) from Ágios Geórgios*

# ÁGIOS GÓRDIS

**(136 A2) (*m* C6) At the south end of Ágios Górdis, a rocky pinnacle rises out of the water like an exclamation mark indicating the beguiling beauty of this long stretch of beach. Striking rock formations on the surrounding cliffs soar up to provide the perfect backdrop for a romantic sunset.**

A blemish on this pristine landscape is the "Pink Palace", the work of an ambitious hotelier which would fit better in Barbie's world than Corfu's coastline. But the building does little to spoil the mood of this tiny resort geared to holidaymakers; just 200 m/650 ft long, its main street is bursting with good bars and tavernas on both sides and you will not find a more compact, lively nightlife anywhere else on the island.

This rocky outcrop is the unofficial landmark of Ágios Górdis

## FOOD & DRINK

### ARK KITCHEN BAR

This casually designed beach bar is the perfect place if you don't plan to move around much on holiday. Have breakfast here before the beach (with free of charge sun loungers and parasols for local guests), followed by a snack for lunch, an ice cream later on in the afternoon and evening meal for sunset. It also hosts live music and rock. If things get wild, you can even spend the night on the beach. *Daily from 9am | in the southern section of the beach | Moderate*

### LINDA'S

Woven backrest chairs, white tablecloths and flowers on the tables. The proprietor Sophia knows what her guests expect. Plates are garnished with sprigs of rosemary, vine leaves and onion rings as a sign of her good taste. Corfiot specialities such as *sofríto* are definitely worth trying here. *Daily, evenings only | on the main road to the beach | Moderate*

## ENTERTAINMENT

### LEMON TREE

Forget yellow; the favourite colours of the proprietors of this trendy cocktail bar are undoubtedly lilac and violet. Run by

### MIKE'S DANCING PUB

Fed up with sitting outside? The resort's only indoor bar gets busy around 10pm, hosting live acts, karaoke every Wednesday and even Beatles revival shows. Music from the 80s fits the retro

Mending fishing nets can be monotonous work, but fun in the right company

a family of four consisting of three bearded brothers Thános, Michális and Geórgios and their long-haired sister Samantha, this open-air bar serves cocktails all with a unique colour and taste. Underneath the shade of the large lemon tree, guests can sit on cosy wooden benches, the more sociable alternative to the bar stools elsewhere, and discuss the difference between lilac and violet... *Daily from 6pm | north of the village road*

vibe of this pub. *Daily from 10pm | at the junction bus stop*

## WHERE TO STAY

### DANDÍDIS

There is no road separating these 14 beachside rooms and apartments from the beach; the breakfast and taverna veranda is the only thing between your bed and the sea. The rooms are 27 m2 in size and the apartments 50 m2; all are well-furnished. The breakfast buffet ranges from yoghurt to bacon. The taverna closes at 10pm so as not to disturb sleeping guests. *14 rooms | middle beach section | tel. 26 61 05 32 32 | www.dandidis.com | Moderate*

## WHERE TO GO

### PARAMÓNAS ⭐
(136 A–B3) *(ⓜ D7)*

This coastal settlement, with only two dozen houses and a 300 m/984 ft-long sand-and-shingle beach, is part of the parish of Ágios Mattheós. People looking for peace and quiet stay in *Paramónas Hotel (22 rooms | tel. 26 61 07 56 95 | www.paramonas-hotel.com | Moderate)* or the modern INSIDER TIP *Skála guesthouse (10 rooms | tel. 26 61 07 50 32 | tel. 26 61 07 51 08 | Moderate)* which has one of the most beautiful gardens on the island and a small pool. The taverns *Plóri (Budget)* and *Sun Set (Budget)* are both of good standard and right on the coast. *13 km (8.1 miles) from Ágios Górdis*

### PENDÁTI
(136 A3) *(ⓜ C–D 6)*

If you stay in Ágios Górdis, you should take the 20–30 minute walk up to the unspoiled mountain village of *Pendáti* at least once. The path winds up the steep coastline through dense green fields, offering contrasting views of the rocky pinnacle and the beach. Drivers can also enjoy the INSIDER TIP panorama over Ágios Górdis from the two terraces at 🍽 *Chris Place (Budget)* is breathtaking. Owner Sofía prepares a freshly made *moussaká* everyday – it's best at lunchtime! *11 km (6.8 miles) from Ágios Górdis by road; only 2 km (1.2 mile) on foot*

# MESSONGÍ-MORAÍTIKA

(136 C3–4) *(ⓜ D7)* **A tiny passenger ferry and a wide road bridge link the coastal resorts of Messongí (pop. 290) and Moraítika (pop. 600). A small river separates the two, which fills the sea with water in summer. An idyllic sight is**

# THE FISH CULT

The Corfiots feel that the sea is the best pantry. At home, they usually eat small, inexpensive fish but when they go out, only the best is good enough. And they always order more than they can eat. Fish is a cult object; it has religious significance as the symbol of Christ and is a healthy food. These are just two reasons that make fish farming one of the most important economic pillars on the Ionian Islands. The more than 500 Greek fish farms even deliver to restaurants and markets in Germany and Italy. Fish that are not to be found in local waters are imported from Thailand, Indonesia and South America. The scampi the Greeks love so much are just as fresh in many countries in northern Europe. If you want to try regional fish, you should limit yourself to small *gópes, gávri* and *marídes*. These are often caught by small trawlers sailing from Corfiot harbours.

the group of fishing and excursion boats mooring at the port of Messongí in front of the estuary.

Otherwise the villages offer little for tourists. Situated to the south of the river, Messongí consists of a row of houses between the promenade and narrow sandy-pebbly beach.

## FOOD & DRINK

### BACCHUS

Small, discreet taverna with its shady, leaf-covered veranda, polyglot proprietor and spotless dining area. Freshly made regional cooking and excellent value for money. *Daily, evenings*

Shark jaws and coral are on display in the small shell museum in Benítses

The more modern Moraítika is divided between its wider stretch of beach lined with hotels and simple beach bars and the busy main road dotted with supermarkets, bars and restaurants. A far more picturesque destination awaits you in the old village of Moraítika on the hill behind the main road with its small choice of pretty tavernas.

*only | in the southern beach section of Messongí | www.bacchus.gr | Budget*

### OLD VILLAGE TAVERNA

This tavern with a flower-adorned terrace is located directly on the tiny village square of old Moraítika. The landlord Níkos takes pleasure in explaining in various languages the Corfiot dishes which his wife prepares and are often served by his daughters. *Daily from 6pm | Budget*

### ZAKS

The chef Zacharías learned his trade in Bern and London. His experience in international gourmet cuisine and gastronomy is clearly evident in this fine-dining restaurant with excellent, yet not pretentious, service and delicious menu. His waiters know how to flambé and Zacharías is no beginner when it comes to vegetarian cooking ever since he cooked a dinner for Prince Charles in London. *Daily, evenings only | Messongí, on the main road near the bridge | Expensive*

## BEACHES

As everywhere else on the east coast, the beaches at Messongí and Moraítika are very narrow, covered in coarse sand and pebbles. Both beaches are extremely crowded. Guests staying at one of the beach hotels in Moraítika often prefer to stay by the pool or in the hotel garden. The water sports station, at the public beach in front of the large Messongí Beach hotel, hires out canoes and peddle boats and organises water-skiing and parasailing.

## ENTERTAINMENT

### GOLDEN BEACH ●

Chrístos would be a serious contender for The X Factor. The beach bar's proprietor is a lively entertainer, hosting a different show every evening in summer. Whether Elvis shows, sirtáki, Latin nights or quiz evenings, Chrístos gets every guest to join in. The audience comes from all over Europe, making the evenings truly memorable. *Shows daily from about 8:30pm | on the beach of Moraítika*

### TIME OUT

Not in a party mood? Relax and unwind from all the partying with the shishas in this small bar. Non-smoker? Then try one of the cocktails such as the "Greek Doctor". Decide for yourself if one's enough or you need two or three to hit the spot. *On Moraítika's main street*

## WHERE TO STAY

**INSIDER TIP ▶ CHRISTINA BEACH**
This small beachside hotel is the closest you will get to living by the sea on Corfu. Your ground-floor room is literally just 20 steps from the water. The owner Dimítris only rents to guests staying a minimum of three nights – but it's definitely worth staying around so long. *16 rooms | Messongí | access also from the coast road | tel. 26 61 07 67 71 | www.hotelchristina.gr | Moderate*

### THREE STARS

A garden dotted with palm trees, a pool almost on the beach, a beach bar on the narrow promenade and breakfast accompanied by sea views. For Moraítika, reason enough to stay especially due to its excellent value for money. *103 rooms | on the beach right north of the large hotel Messongí Beach | tel. 26 61 07 52 63 | www.corfu3starshotel.com | Budget–Moderate*

## WHERE TO GO

### BENÍTSES
(136 C2) (*Ø D6*)

Napoleon was a shell collector. He presents his collection in his purpose-built ● *Shell Museum (March–Oct daily 10am–6pm | admission 4 euros | northern part of the coastal road | www.corfushellmuseum.com)* that is better signposted than any other attraction on Corfu. Inside, owner

Napoleon Sagiás often guides his visitors himself and explains shells from all over the world as well as sharks' jaws and coral. Apart from that, there's not much to this place which is usually advertised a bit too positively – too many people crowding the small beach and in the centre the scant remains (freely accessible) of small Roman baths from the 2nd century AD. *8 km (5 miles) from Messongí*

### BÚKARI
(137 D4) (*ⅅ E7*)

For a long time the small fishing port of Boúkari (pop. 50) was home to just one fish taverna: *Karídis (daily | Expensive)*. The eatery was so good that it attracted more and more guests, including celebrities. Others followed suite and today there are over half a dozen good fish tavernas well-spaced along the road between the port and Messongí. Every guest has found their favourite. *6 km (3.7 miles) from Messongí*

### CHLÓMOS ★
(136 C4) (*ⅅ E 7*)

Normally, pretty mountain viallges are more characteristic of the island's north. Chlómos has only 700 inhabitants and is one of the loveliest mountain villages in the south of the island.The tiers of old houses are arranged in the shape of an amphitheatre on the green hills around linked together by a labyrinth of narrow lanes and steps. Most of these dwellings stand empty except for in the summer months. There are two good tavernas at both entrances to the village to welcome thirsty tourists every day. ᐳᐸ *Panórama (daily | Budget)* is to the south and has the more picturesque view over the village while ᐳᐸ INSIDER TIP *Bális (daily | Budget)* in the north attracts guests with delicious food and splendid coastal and sea panorama. *5 km (3.1 miles) from Messongí*

### PETRÍTI
(137 D4) (*ⅅ E7*)

Why do Egyptians come to Corfu? For a holiday if they are millionaires or to be hired as fishermen if they are struggling to survive back home. They work on the large fishing boats, like the ones you see daily in the port of Petrítí, carefully mending the fishing nets. Their catch of the day is then served in the fish tavernas along the port. Petrítí mainly attracts independent travellers, which is not a bad thing.

# ESOTERIC CENTRES

● Many centres offer courses, seminars and workshops throughout the six summer months. At the *Ouranos Centre (www.ouranosclub.de)* in Ágios Stéfanos Avliotón the focus is on meditation and creative programmes, while the more international *Alexis Zorbas Centre (Arillás | www.alexiszorbas. com)* stresses body work. The *Corfu Buddha Hall (www.corfubuddhahall.com)* in Magoulades offers a wide range of workshops, events and programs on meditation and body awareness. The *Manto Center (Ágios Geórgios | www. manto-corfu.com)* villa with a 6000 m² (64,583 sq. ft) large garden has been designed by artists and offers yoga courses and intensive workshops.

Paradise in the Panórama garden – delicious food and hammock for relaxing

A strange rock with three crosses and the Greek and Byzantine flags lies just off the narrow beach of the town. A former local policeman, who often sits on a self-made raft near the island and sings, erected them along with a small model of a church. This is to remind people that the small island was once the site of a church dedicated to St Nicholas that is, today, completely in ruins.

The 70 m/230 ft long, sandy *Nótos Beach* lies on the other side of the rocky island at the south end of the village and is prettier than the town beach. If you don't enjoy sand, spend a relaxing day in the ● INSIDER TIP *garden of the Panórama taverna (tel. 26 62 05 17 07 | www.panoramacorfu.gr | tavern Moderate | apartments Budget)* on the other side of the headland. Surrounded by banana plants and blossoming shrubs, yucca palms and flowers, you can lie back and relax on the sun loungers and beach chairs dotted around the garden. There is also a wooden jetty to help bathers access the water.

The owners Thanássis Vagiás and his wife Ina prepare deliciously aromatic Greek specialities, making it even more difficult to prise yourself away from this idyllic spot. If you don't want to leave, the family also rents 15 spacious apartments in the middle of olive groves about 150 m/360 ft away from the taverna. *15 km (9.3 miles) from Messongí*

## VRAGANIOTIKA (136 B4) (*ロ D7*)

How is oil extracted from the olives? This question and more are answered on a guided tour of the *Olive Oil Factory* owned by Spíros and Vangélis Mavroúdis. Built in 1993, the factory houses ultra-modern equipment. In contrast, the *open-air museum* next door shows visitors how difficult it was to extract the oil over the last centuries. You can try, and of course, buy all the oils at the end of the tour. *Mon–Sat 8:30am–8pm, Sun 9am–1pm | admission free | on the man road in the direction of Lefkími | 3 km (1.9 mile) from Messongí*

# CENTRAL CORFU

Do you need the smell of town air once in a while to stop you suffocating in the tourist enclaves? But you still like to swim and sunbathe? Then central Corfu is the perfect destination for you. From early morning to late in the evening, affordable bus services run between nearly all the resorts and the island capital, even a taxi will not cost you the earth.

Most of the island's large, luxury hotels are located in the broad bay between Kérkyra and Dassiá. But, only the birds see that. Even the larger complexes are well hidden between lush greenery, or separated from each other by gently rolling hills or coastal bays. Here, you will be able to spend your holidays in park-like surroundings on the seashore. Most of the beaches are narrow and usually peb-

bly, but the hotels offset this with spacious, beautiful sunbathing lawns and pool terraces. The sheltered bays are particularly attractive for waterskiing and paragliding. The beaches slope gradually into the water and are well suited for children (with bathing shoes) and many hotels and water-sport facilities have built wooden jetties that can be used for sunbathing. If you want to take a swim, ladders make it easier to access deeper water directly.

The west coast in central Corfu is completely different in character to the eastern side of the island. Lovely old villages like Pélekas – once a favourite among the hippie crowd in its day and still a popular destination for backpackers now – and Sinirádes nestle on the hills further inland and there are

From a former hippie spot to up-market holiday area: swimming during the day and a visit to the island's capital at night

a number of no-through-roads that wind their way down to long, wide sandy beaches. Hotel settlements such as Glífada and Érmones, with its good water sports centre, diving school and the only golf course on the Ionian Islands, have sprung up at the ends of these beaches. There is still no tarmac road, only a gruelling dirt and cement path, down to the beach at Mirtiótis. The only substantial building as such near the beach is a monastery – the other end is particularly popular among nudists.

# DAFNÍLA & DASSIÁ

**(135 D4)** *(⚏ C4)* **The Club Med in the north of the green bay of Dassiá finally closed its doors in 2002. Hard to imagine now the crowds of affluent French tourists who spent their holidays on this peninsula for over 50 years living in Polynesian style huts, walking around half-naked and paying for drinks and**

**food with glass beads. The journey originally took two and a half days from Paris, via Venice to Corfu by train and ferry.**

The larger *Dafníla* peninsula on the other side of the bay has since evolved into an of its romantic setting surrounded by cacti, agaves and flowers; the residing priest is very friendly and allows guests to use the surrounding gardens for the wedding celebrations afterwards. It's also

Picturesquely surrounded by water: The small church in Ipapánti in the south of Dafníla

exclusive holiday resort for the wealthy. Even the Russian billionaire Roman Abramovich bought an estate there. The northern part of the peninsula today resembles a jungle dotted with the remains of straw huts. Situated between the two extremes is the resort of Dassiá which has remained relatively normal. The island's main road cuts directly through the centre, leaving behind an uninspiring thoroughfare lined with bars and shops. A nicer place to spend the evening is at the beach with its lively beach bars and tavernas.

## SIGHTSEEING

### IPAPÁNTI CHURCH ★

Many couples tie the knot in this quaint church on the tiny island not just because worth taking the detour from the main road to visit this church (built in 1713) on days when there are no wedding ceremonies. *Daily from noon | follow the small signpost to Koméno on the main island road*

## FOOD & DRINK

### ETRUSCO

Gastronomic guides describe Ettore Botrini's restaurant as the "avant-garde of Greek gastronomy", the best restaurant on any Greek island and the second best in the whole country. He is a disciple of the revolutionary "technomotion" style developed by Spain's star chef Andoni Luis Aduriz: He does not sell food but emotions; he doesn't nourish the stomach but the soul. The menu changes often and has offered such delicacies as medallions of fish in triple-sec with sesame, lamb simmered with cumquats and olive-oil or tomato ice-cream. In spite of his fame, set meals are available from as low as 60 euros. *May–Oct; daily, evenings only | on the road from Dassiá to Áno Korakianá | tel. 26 61 09 33 42 | Expensive*

### KARIDIÁ 😊

If you prefer a more down-to-earth Greek taverna which doesn't cost the earth, try the "walnut tree" restaurant. Surrounded by splendid landscape, you can sit on the veranda and be served Greek dishes and tasty salads freshly prepared every day by the owner's family. The house wine is pleasant and most of the vegetables come from their own gardens; vegetarians will love it here. *Daily, evenings only | Dassiá | on the main road | Moderate*

### MALIBU BEACH CLUB

This beach club caters to avid sun worshippers, serving snacks (ranging from toast to grilled octopus) to the sun loungers on the beach, lawn or at the poolside. A glass of champagne can also be ordered to accompany the evening sunset. *Daily | between the hotels Dassia Beach and Dassia Chandris | Budget*

## SPORTS & BEACHES

The only beach worth mentioning on the Komméno Peninsula occupied by Dafníla is near the Hotel Corfu Imperial. The main, mostly pebbly beach at Dassiá is around 700 m/2,296 ft long. There is no beach road to disturb your bathing in the midst of verdant nature. The quiet *Ágios Nikólaos Beach* between Dassiá and Dafníla has a 300 m/984 ft stretch of sand. It is also the site of the – easily recognisable – country estate of the Russian oligarch Roman Abramovich, one of the world's richest men. There are often even two large motor yachts anchored in front of his high-security residence.

There are three good water sports centres on the main beach in Dassiá with two others on the hotel beaches at Daphníla Bay and Corfu Imperial.

## ENTERTAINMENT

### EDEM BEACH NIGHTCLUB

Full moon or underground parties, retro sounds from the 1960s-90s and rock: there is always something going on

⭐ **Ipapánti Church**
Just as photogenic, but not as well-known as the one famous Mouse Island → p. 82

⭐ **Kaizer's Throne**
A majestic place to watch the sun set → p. 89

⭐ **Sandy beach at Mirtiótissa**
Paradise – bathe like Adam and Eve on the 300 m/984 ft-long sandy beach → p. 90

⭐ **Levant**
The hotel with its unique hillside location offers rooms with panoramic views → p. 91

⭐ **Folklore Museum in Sinarádes**
In this museum you can see how the Corfiots used to live – and enjoy local specialities in a traditional *kafenío* in the charming mountain village → p. 93

**MARCO POLO HIGHLIGHTS**

between the end of May and September at one of the island oldest beach clubs. "Party until you drop" is the motto here. Admission is free and if temperatures get too hot, you can cool down in the sea just a stone's throw away. *Daily | Dassiá | in front of the Hotel Schería, approx. 100 m/328 ft north of the Eléa Beach hotel*

### TARTAYA

Lit up in colour and wrapped in colourful fabrics, the palm trees in this exotic lounge bar are in all shades, except green. Only Ikea has a wider choice of lounge furniture and seating. Singles can make themselves comfortable on one of the high bar stools at the bar. The resident DJ plays all the latest sounds. *Daily | Dassiá | on the main road north of the Chandris Hotel*

## WHERE TO STAY

INSIDER TIP ▶ **DASSIÁ BEACH**

You cannot get any closer to the beach than at the Dassiá Beach hotel, separated only from the sea by its shaded veranda. The tastefully decorated rooms with balconies are only 10 m (33ft) away from the water's edge and the sounds of the sea will send you off to sleep. The hotel has an extremely laid-back atmosphere and the owner's family makes sure you have everything you need for a pleasant stay. The hotel has a bathing jetty and the next water sports centre is only 50 m/164 ft away; the main street with its cafés and bars, approximately 300 m/984 ft. *54 rooms | Dassiá | on the main beach | tel. 26 61 09 32 24 | www. dassiahotels.gr | Moderate*

### NEFÉLI ☼

Some like the beach for its scorching hot temperatures. Others prefer lounging under the shade of the olive trees away from the intense sun. If you belong to the latter group, then the Nefelí hotel is perfect for you. Housing just 45 rooms, this hotel is more like a large villa and although they are small, all rooms are individually furnished; you can even spend the night in their special Odysseus or Sisi themed rooms. The closest sandy beach is 800 m/2,625 ft away on foot. *Komméno Peninsula | tel. 26 61 09 10 33 | www.hotelnefeli.com | Moderate*

## WHERE TO GO

### ÁNO KORAKIÁNA
(134 C3) (*Ø C 3–4*)

If you want to experience authentic village life untouched by tourism, then head to the large inland villages of Áno and Káto, upper and lower Korakianá, with their 2000 inhabitants and 37 (usually closed) churches and chapels. Visit the villages in the late afternoon from 5:30pm onwards when the Venetian houses and narrow lanes come to life. Once the temperatures have begun to cool, children come out to play, teenagers gather on the streets and women sit gossiping in front of their houses while their men go off to play cards in the local *kafenío*.

The sculptor Aristidis Metallinós (1908–87) is not part of this anymore. He once frequented these streets and even owned a nice museum on the main street of Áno Korakiána. Unfortunately he didn't leave behind enough money for an attendant which is why the museum is closed. Some of his works can be seen hanging from the house and sitting on the roof.

In contrast the *Aléxandros-Soútzos-Museum (Mon, thu, Sat, Sun 8:30am–3:30pm, Wed, Fri 10am–2pm and 6pm–9pm | admission 2 euros | www.corfu.*

The chairs are waiting! After the steep drive up, you've earned a refreshment in Sokráki

*nationalgallery.gr)* in Káto Korakianáis open on a regular basis. It belongs to the Greek National Gallery in Athens and exhibits some spectacular Greek art from the 18th century to today. Some of the works would not look out of place in your own living room. The museum is housed in a medieval building with tower, once a noble guesthouse and then a hotel. The likes of Kaiser Wilhelm II, Greek kings, the billionaire shipping magnate Aristotélis Onássis and his operatic diva Maria Callas have all stayed here. So switch your smartphone on and relive the amazing voice of this opera singer. *4/6 km (2.5/3.7 miles) from Dassiá*

## ÍPSOS & PIRGI
### (135 D3–4) *(ⓜ C4)*

These two coastal resorts merge into one another and are examples of undesirable developments in tourism. Holiday-makers sun themselves on the – at most – 5 m/ 16.5 ft-wide strip of shingles directly below the busy main island road; the other side of the road is lined with mediocre bars, restaurants, souvenir shops and roads to the camping sites. However, there is one culinary bright spot: the INSIDER TIP **Le Grand Balcon** restaurant *(daily | north of Ípsos above the road to Barbáti | Moderate)* that serves mostly specialities from the north of mainland Greece. Here, *chtapódi*, octopus, is still prepared as the typical Corfiot *bourdétto*. Another highlight for connoisseurs is *katsikáki gástras*, kid (of the goat variety!) cooked in a clay pot. In winter, wild boar is served. *2 km (1.2 mile) from Dassiá*

## INSIDER TIP SOKRÁKI ☼
### (134 C3) *(ⓜ C3)*

Driving to Sokráki is quite an experience if you take the road from Áno Korakiána.

The tarmac road is mostly only single-lane and winds itself like a corkscrew up a steep slope with 23 hairpin bends and even more gentle ones revealing breathtaking views of central and southern Corfu. Luckily there are several passing places where you can stop and also take pictures of the raod or the great views. The passengers usually have sweaty hands when they finally reach Sokráki and the driver will need to shake out his arms after all the hard work. The best place to do that is on the tiny village square where two unspoilt *kafenía* serve refreshing drinks and snacks. *11 km (6.8 miles) from Dassiá*

# GUVIÁ & KONTOKÁLI

**(135 D5)** *(C–D 4)* **The total cost of all 960 yachts in the marina at Guviá (pop. 950) would probably exceed the GDP of some third-world countries. The Latin phrase "Suum cuique", or "to each what he deserves" apparently only applies to some.**

The marina is however open to the public for visitors to get a closer look at all the wealth on show. Things have not changed since Venetian times: In the late 18th century, northern Italians would bring their galleons to be repaired and housed over winter in the old Venetian shipyards. The ships were not powered by sails but by slaves who proved far more reliable than the wind. The wind is still a rare guest in *Kontokáli* (pop. 1600).

Merging together along the coast, the neighbouring villages are situated on a bay that is almost secluded from the sea. Looking through the gap out to sea, the landscape may remind you of Switzerland with the high mountains of Albania and the Greek mainland in the distance which are usually covered with snow between November and March.

### SIGHTSEEING

#### VENETIAN SHIPYARDS

Today, the walls, arches and entrance portal of the shipyard constructed in 1778 seem out of place and rather neglected; however, these buildings, which are now in ruins, were full of life in the last 20 years of Venetian dominance over Corfu. This is where ships were built, repaired and put into dry dock over winter. *Free access | between the main beach and marina, well* signposted in the village ("Venetian ship-yards")

## FOOD & DRINK

### INSIDER TIP ROÚLA ✕

Celebrities like to head off to far-flung places away from the madding crowds. Rather than idyllic spots, they are simply looking for somewhere to escape

same peninsula as the Hotel Kontokáli Bay that is signposted on the main road | *Expensive*

### TÁKIS

Many of the guests find the restaurant proprietor eccentric yet not unfriendly. He has original ideas which he likes to incorporate into his menu. The favourites are grilled dishes, but regulars go

It has been a long time since ships were built here: the Venetian shipyards in Guviá

their hectic lives. Roúla is this type of place. Located in a side arm of the bay with views over the yacht harbour and mountains, this large fish taverna lies far away from any tourist centre. Workers are busy in the shipyards on the opposite side of the bay. Mikhail Gorbachev, Nana Mouskouri, Vicky Leandros and many other VIPs came here not to bathe (the water does not invite you to swim) but for the excellent fish and seafood. *Daily, evenings only; Sat & Sun also open for lunch | on the*

for his home-smoked trout from the Greek mainland and his rabbit is almost as good, if not better than the *kokorétsi*, grilled lamb offal wrapped in natural skin and grilled on the spit. *Daily; usually closed in the afternoon in July and August | Moderate*

## BEACHES

The most beautiful beach in *Kontokáli* is located directly in front of the Hotel Kontokáli Bay and, like all other beaches in Greece, is open to the public. All of the other beaches between Kontokáli and Guviá were sacrificed for the construction of the marina. *Guviá* now only has a 200 m/656 ft-long main beach and a strip beneath the Louis Corcyra Beach Hotel; both are mostly pebbly.

## ENTERTAINMENT

### O2

This place probably won't take your breath away but this attractive bar is the coolest in the resort. On the village road between Gouviá and Marina. *Daily | village road in the direction of Kontokáli*

## WHERE TO STAY

### CASA LUCIA

Looking for something out of the ordinary? Then stay at one of the stone cottages owned by Val Osborne-Androutsopoulou and her daughter Zoe. Dating back to Venetian times, these cottages have been restored with red tiles on the roof and wooden beams under the roof. The pool is embedded in a tropical garden full of grass and blossoming flowers. All ground-floor apartments are robustly furnished and have fully-equipped kitchens. A taverna serving vegan food is situated just 300 m/990 ft from the cottages and the next beach is 3 km/1.8 mile away. You can take part in yoga, tai-chi and qigong courses several times a week – and the seminar room can be booked for your own workshops. *10 rooms | Sgombroú | to the left 150 m/492 ft off the national road from Dassiá to Paleokastrítsa | tel. 26 61 09 14 19 | www.casa-lucia-corfu.com | Moderate*

### KONTOKÁLI BAY

If price is not an issue, then book into this large five-storey hotel. The green lawns hide from view the mass of concrete – most of the roof is also covered in grass. The hotel offers amazing, unspoilt views and a prime position on a small peninsula just 6 km/3.7 miles from the island capital yet far away from other hotels. Mountain bikes are available for hire – why not try cycling into Corfu Town? *259 rooms | Kontokáli | tel. 26 61 09 05 00 | www.kontokalibay.com | Expensive*

## WHERE TO GO

### ÁGIOS IOÁNNIS
(135 D5) (*ØD5*)

If you blink on driving through Ágios Ioánnis, you'll probably miss it. Most visitors usually head straight for the *Aqualand* (see page 117) water park at the northern end of the village. Yet the village's old historical centre also offers good accommodation. The garden of the INSIDER TIP *Pension Marída (13 rooms | tel. 26 61 05 24 10 | Budget)* on the village square was once a popular campsite back in the days of backpacking tourism and the old owner has managed to stay young at heart. Small groups of hikers or bikers sometimes stay in this country house dating from 1823. The guesthouse feels like a home from home and guests enjoy eating with locals in the taverna opposite. You will find it hard to get around if you don't have a car or bike. *5 km (3.1 miles) from Guviá*

# PÉLEKAS, GLIFÁDA & MIRTIÓTISSA

(134–135 C–D6) (*ØC5*) **The large mountain village Pélekas (pop. 565) has lost**

The church and taverna are at the heart of every Corfiot village: evening in Pélekas

its flair over the years. Just ten years ago, the walls were covered in artistic graffiti on hundreds of metres and a large international street art festival was held here every year. These days are gone and the village only attracts those in search of nostalgia and romance.

The village's scene has gradually relocated to the *Glifáda Beach* (2 km/0.8 mile) in summer. In the days where there were no hotels along the sea front, backpackers were shuttled down to the seaside by bus. Today the beach is firmly in the grip of mass tourism and the newly built hotel complexes try to keep guests on their sites. Despite of this, Pélekas is still worth a visit if only to watch the sun set behind the hillside rather than into the sea.

## SIGHTSEEING

### KAIZER'S THRONE ★ ☆

During his stays on Corfu, the German Kaiser Wilhelm II was fond of a small rock on the top of the hill *(Sunset Point)* that towers above Pélekas where he sat and watched the sun set. Today you can drive up here from the village following the signs along the tarmac road and toast the sunset with a cocktail from the hotel bar. This natural spectacle is particularly special in June. Then, it looks like a red ball of fire is rolling down the Corfiot hills when the sun seems to settle on a mountain top before continuing on its heavenly journey at the same angle as the slope.

### PANAGÍA MIRTIÓTISSA (MONÍ MYRTIDIÓN) MONASTERY

Just 200 m (650 ft) from the nudist beaches of Mirtiótissa, one of the most beautifully located monasteries on the island lies hidden between olive trees, banana plants and countless flowers. According to legend, a Turk who had converted to Christianity founded it in the 14th century after he had discovered an icon of Maria in a myrtle bush. However, the present buildings date from the 19th century.

Today, just one monk lives in the monastery; he keeps it in order and would like to revitalise the old oil mill. *Daily 9am–1pm and 5–9pm | access via a narrow road, which is tarmaced at first and then cemented, that is off the road between Pélekas and the Rópa Valley; it is easy to miss the signpost! | car park (chargeable) half way up; limited parking on the beach and near the monastery*

## FOOD & DRINK

### LEVANT ⚜

The views and the scenery are as typical as the food on your plate. *Sofríto, pastitsáda* and rabbit-*Stifádo* are just as good as the *soufikó*, a sort of strictly vegetarian ratatouille which is seldom on any menu. Those with a sweet tooth can order the fitting dessert, an oriental *kataífi* or *baklavá*. After that, you're sure to have sweet dreams. *Terrace all day; restaurant daily, evenings only | reservation recommended: tel. 26 61 09 42 30 | Expensive*

## SPORS & BEACHES

The secluded, approximately 300 m/984 ft-long, ⭐ *sandy beach at Mirtiótissa* is unofficially used as a nudist

Not a bad job: lifeguard on Glifáda Beach – it's only stressful during the crowded peak season

beach. So far, only a limited number of sun beds and umbrellas have been available for hire but there is a certain amount of shade among the rocks. This beach is really something and well worth visiting, no matter where you are staying on Corfu.

*Glifáda Beach*, on the other hand, is usually very crowded but there are plenty of sun beds, umbrellas and water sports activities. Two narrow tarmac roads lead down to *Pélekas Beach* which is 500 m/1,640 ft long, not quite as busy and also suitable for children. There is a water-sport centre here too.

The only way to reach all three beaches from Pélekas is down the steep road on foot or by car; an off-road vehicle is required for the route down to the Mirtiótissa beach. Despite this, the beach is often well visited.

## ENTERTAINMENT

The nightlife is concentrated in the cafes and bars around the village square and surrounding alleyways.

### PÉLEKAS CAFÉ ☼

This modern café on the small main square is a meeting place for the locals and holidaymakers in the evening. The village priest even drops by regularly. There is Greek and international music and you have a good view of the island through the wide-open windows. The visitors' book is always open too and is full of praise for the friendly atmosphere. *Daily | Pélekas*

### ZANSI BAR

This tiny music bar has not changed since it opened in 1980: crowds of guests gather inside and outside to drink and chat all year round. The dancing starts at the latest when rock 'n' roll

is played. *Daily from 9pm at the earliest | on the village square*

## WHERE TO STAY

### LEVANT ★ ☼

You can reach for the skies in Hotel Levant. Perched on the hillside above the village, the hotel is housed in a splendid villa. Watch the fantastic sunset over the Kaizer's Throne from your private balcony and relax and unwind during the day in the hotel's garden with small pool. *25 rooms | Pélekas | Sunset Point | tel. 26 61 09 42 30 | www.levantcorfu.com | Expensive*

### INSIDER TIP ► PÉLEKAS COUNTRY CLUB

A former Venetian manor secluded away from tourism and traffic is aimed at those looking for unique, luxurious accommodation on Corfu. Stables and other courtyard buildings have been transformed into spacious, ground-floor apartments decorated with antique furniture; the president suite in the main building has even accommodated the French President François Mitterrand and the Greek Prime Minister Geórgios Papandréou. The club's pool and bar are located in luxurious parkland. Guests are served breakfast on the long table on the main building's ground floor where they can also relax or play billiards. The hotel also has its own helipad. *10 rooms | km 8 on the road from Kérkyra to Pélekas | tel. 26 61 05 29 18 | www. country-club.gr | Expensive*

### INSIDER TIP ► PENSION MARTINI (TÉLLIS AND BRIGITTE)

The German-Greek hosts and their sons, Spíros and Níkos, take exceptional care of their guests. They will gladly join you for a glass of wine or ouzo and sometimes let you help at the barbecue. ☼

The rooms at the back of the house offer a beautiful view over the island. Hikers on the Corfu Trail are given special discounts! *8 rooms | Pélekas | in the centre, signposted on the main road | tel. 26 61 09 43 26 | www.pensionmartini.com | Budget*

### THOMAS HOTEL

Two Italian brothers run this well-established guesthouse in a relaxed manner. All the rooms have balconies and the owners have set up an Italian-Greek restaurant on the ground floor that is open in the high season. *16 rooms | on the road to Kaizer's Throne | tel. 26 61 03 09 44 | Budget*

## WHERE TO GO

### ÉRMONES
(134 C5–6) (*ʃ C5*)

Today, as in ancient times, Homer's Odysseus would certainly rub his eyes in disbelief, awakening out of a deep sleep on the beach at Érmones after his 10-year journey home. Maybe he would see a bathing beauty as lovely as Nausicaa, the daughter of King Alcinous of Phaeacia, standing in front of him. However, he would certainly not recognise the surroundings. The hinterland is now covered with a sprawl of hotels and guesthouses. Odysseus would be equally surprised to see the funicular that ferries guests staying at the *Grand Mediterraneo Resort Hotel* from their rooms high up on the slope down to the beach, which – at just 200 m/656 ft long – is not really one of Corfu's most beautiful. However, the sports possibilities near the hotels are good and varied. More attractively priced accommodation can be found at *Hotel Elena (30 rooms | tel. 2661 09 41 31 | www.hotelelena.gr | Moderate)*. *7 km (4.3 miles) from Pélekas*

### RÓPA VALLEY
(136 C4–5) (*ʃ C 4–5*)

Ever wondered what attracts so many people to the game of golf? Then spend a few hours watching the golfers from Corfu golf club's restaurant veranda (open to the public) and you may learn why. You will feel as if you are in an

# VERSATILE LITTLE ORANGES

● Corfu's most famous speciality is the cumquat *(koum kouát)*. Corfu is the only place in Europe where they are grown as a cash crop. The fruit – which is the size of a small plum and originally came from China – was first brought to the island by the British in the first half of the 19th century. Like oranges, they mature in winter and can be picked between January and March. Corfiot companies use them to make various liqueurs: a colour-less one from the flesh of the fruit and one that is bright pink from the skins. Cumquats are often made into jam, sold candied and can be eaten fresh during the harvest. The skin can be eaten as well; it gives the fruit its tangy aroma. If you want to see how these fruits grow on Corfu, you can best do so by driving to *Nímfes* (see p. 53) in the north of the island where particularly many of these trees thrive.

You are treated to contrasting views of the crystal-clear waters in the mountain village Sinarádes

English landscaped park. The small modern chapel next to it is the only hint that you are actually in Greece. *6 km (3.7 miles) from Pélekas*

## SINARÁDES
### (136 A2) (*ʍ C6*)

Do you know what a birthing chair is? The ⭐ *Folklore Museum (Mon–Sat 9am–2pm | admission 2 euros | signposted at the church; leave your vehicle at the car park in the village centre)* in Sinarádes (pop. 1120) owns two of them. The exhibition on the two floors of this historical building, which was occupied as a house until 1970, shows how the Corfiots lived and worked in the country between 1860 and 1960. There are excellent descriptions of all the exhibits in English. Among the unique objects to be seen are the two birth chairs and figures for the Greek shadow play *karagióssi*.

It is worth taking a short stroll through the village with its many old houses after you have visited the museum. Those that are almost completely overgrown with flowers are particularly lovely. If you want to soak up the down-to-earth, local atmosphere, have a drink in one of the old-fashioned grocery stores-cum-*kafenía* on the road and watch village life go by. One of it is *Sinarádes (Budget)* right on the platía that also serves as the village's parking lot. Stelíos, the proprietor, used to be a sailor and now organises the barbeque for his guests in the evening. In the high season, a lamb is roasted on a spit on Sundays. *6 km (3.7 miles) from Pélekas*

# DISCOVERY TOURS

## ① CORFU AT A GLANCE

**START:** ① Kérkyra
**END:** ① Kérkyra

2 days
Driving time
(without stops)
4.5 hours

**Distance:**
📍 225 km/140 miles

**WHAT TO PACK:** swimwear, hiking boots, sun protection

**IMPORTANT TIPS:** : If you are based in Kérkyra or between Dassiá, Glifáda, Ágios Górdis and Messóngi-Moraítika, you can return to your holiday accommodation to spend the evening of the first day.

Corfu has just too much to see for it to be explored in one day. On this two-day tour, which begins in the capital and takes you to both the island's north and south, you will reach the island's highest point by car and discover its wild, steep coastlines and fantastic beaches.

Would you like to explore the places that are unique to this island? Then the Discovery Tours are just the thing for you – they include terrific tips for stops worth making, breathtaking places to visit, selected restaurants and fun activities. It's even easier with the Touring App: download the tour with map and route to your smartphone using the QR Code on pages 2/3 or from the website address in the footer below – and you'll never get lost again even when you're offline.

→ p. 2/3

**TOURING APP**

In the tiny, centuries-old inland villages, you can expect to find splendid cafés, tavernas and idyllic village squares. Pass through olive-tree forests, explore castles and see the many different faces of Corfu as this tour takes you from one viewpoint to the next along the island's twisting roads.

**09:00am** The tour starts in ❶ **Kérkyra** → p. 32, continues on past the holiday resorts of Kontokáli, Guviá and Dassiá to Pírgi. Drive from Pírgi along the coastal road and turn up a **narrow, twisting road with hairpin bends to Spartilás. Shortly before reaching Sgourádes, head right** up to the

**DAY 1**

❶ Kérkyra 🚌

30 km/18.5 mi

Finiq Mesopotam

Sarandë

SHQIPËRIA

Erikoússa
Erikoússa

Mathráki

Avliótes
Sidári  Róda
Karoussádes
Kavadádes

Anaharávi
Pantokrátor
906

Butrint 825

Parku Kombëtar
i Butrintit

Mathráki
Ákra
Kefalí
Afiónas
Pági
Makrádes

Skriperó
Ípsos

Nissáki
Kassiópi

Çiflik

Kérkira
Κέρκυρα

Ormós
Sagiádas

Kérkira

Giannádes
Pélekas
Gastoúri
Ahélion
576

CFU

Ágios Matthéos

Moraïtika
Messóngi

Messavríssi
Argirádes
Perivóli

Lefkímmi

Kávos

Akrotíri
Asprókavos

8 km
4.97 mi

② Strinílas

5 km/3.1 mi

③ Pantokrátor

27 km/16.8 mi

④ Canal d'Amour

5 km/3.1 mi

tranquil mountain village of ② **Strinílas** → **p. 56**, where you can take a break on the village square under the shade of its ancient elm tree. Now **head up to** ③ **Pantokrátor** → **p. 54**, the island's highest point standing 906 m/2972 ft high. The panoramic view over the island and far into the Albanian and Northern Greek mountains is breathtaking.

After attempting to turn your vehicle around on the narrow mountain ridge (which could prove to be a rather hair-raising experience!), **drive down to the northern coast and take a left on the road around the island.** You will pass the holiday resorts of Acharavi and Róda, and at **Sidári** → **p. 55** treat yourself to a dip in the ④ **Canal** d'Amour → p. 56 before **continuing in the direction of Peruládes.** Plan first a quick **detour to** ⑤ **Cape Drástis** → p. 55 and then stop for lunch in one of the two tavernas at the steep harbour in ⑥ **Peruládes** → p. 55.

**02:00pm** The route then **passes Avliótes to the beach of Ágios Stéfanos and further up through Arillás** to ⑦ **Afiónas** → p. 56. Drive up to the village's church where this road will then end. On the square itself, you can buy excellent-quality INSIDER TIP Corfiot olive oil. Follow the street on the left of the olive oil shop a few steps further to two tavernas which both offer excellent views of the bays of Aríllas and Ágios Geórgios.

Then **cross Ágios Geórgios North** via ⑧ **Pági** with its **Spiros Bond 008 Cafe**, where Roger Moore spent his time during takes of the 1979 James Bond film "For your eyes only". Then carry on **to Makrádes** and the castle ⑨ **Angelókastro** → p. 66. After a 10-minute steep uphill march on foot, you will reach the top with a splendid view along the wild, steep coastline. Then enjoy an afternoon coffee on one of the restaurants' terraces in ⑩ **Lákones** → p. 66, which resemble balconies in the sky, and from which there is a wonderful view

⑤ Cape Drástis

1 km/0.6 mi

⑥ Peruládes

12 km/7.5 mi

⑦ Afiónas

7 km/4.5 mi

⑧ Pági

7 km/4.5 mi

⑨ Angelókastro

4 km/2.5 mi

⑩ Lákones

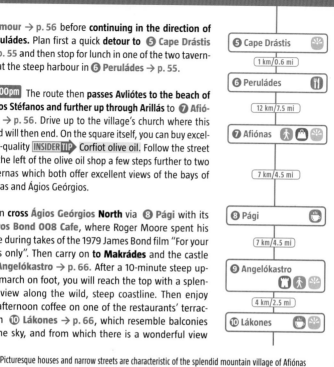

Picturesque houses and narrow streets are characteristic of the splendid mountain village of Afiónas

down to the olive trees and cypresses on **Paleokastrítsa**
→ **p. 63.** For many Corfiots, this is the most beautiful place on earth. It's now too late to visit the monastery so plan to return another day to explore it in peace (can be reached by bus). **Now turn left immediately on entering Paleokastrítsa and then a right straight afterwards** through the lush green Rópa Valley and the large mountain village of ⑪ **Pélekas** → **p. 88.** You will probably reach the village in time to watch the sunset from the **Kaizer's Throne** → **p. 89.** In the evening, you can either eat up here or head down to one of the tavernas in the village of Pélekas. The village also offers basic and affordable accommodation if you do not want to return to your holiday hotel for the night.

**09:00am** Start the next day by **driving from Pélekas to ⑫ Sinarádes** → **p. 93** with its very picturesque road which takes you through the village and to the rustic **snack bar Locanda** on the village square. It is worth visiting the village's **folklore museum.** On the **drive down to ⑬ Ágios Górdis** → **p. 73** take in one of the island's most beautiful coastal landscapes. **Shortly after Ágios Górdis, a narrow tarmac road branches off at a right angle to the village of ⑭ Pendáti** → **p. 75** where you can enjoy your second coffee break of the morning accompanied with a panoramic view on the **Chris Place** terrace. **The narrow, bendy road continues on** through an INSIDER TIP enchanted forest full of century-old olive trees **close to the coast to ⑮ Paramónas** → **p. 75** – an excellent spot for a swim. Follow the road through the enchanted forest to the important fortification of ⑯ **Gardíki** → **p. 72** dating back to the 13th century. The route then turns **to the coast** through vineyards and meadows of cut flowers to ⑰ **Lake Koríssion** → **p. 69** with long, thin stretches of dunes in front of it. **Alonáki** taverna, located at the northern end of the lake in **Chalikúnas,** is a good place to eat lunch in this green paradise.

**02:00pm** Now drive past the castle of Gardíki again and **inland around Lake Korísssíon** to the resort of ⑱ **Ágios Geórgios South** → **p. 68,** which stretches along the sea for almost 3 km/1.9 miles with an INSIDER TIP **amazing dune landscape.** The main road brings you to the small town of ⑲ **Lefkími** → **p. 72,** where you should definitely plan a small detour to the picturesque **river port.** On your way back north, **exit the island's main road near**

---

## Itinerary markers (left column)

( 20 km/12.5 mi )

⑪ Pélekas 🍴🛏

**DAY 2**

( 7 km/4.5 mi )

⑫ Sinarádes ☕🏛

( 4 km/2.5 mi )

⑬ Ágios Górdis ☕

( 4 km/2.5 mi )

⑭ Pendáti ☕☕

( 8 km/5 mi )

⑮ Paramónas 🌊

( 6 km/3.7 mi )

⑯ Gardíki 🏰

( 3 km/1.9 mi )

⑰ Lake Koríssion 🌳☕

( 16 km/10 mi )

⑱ Ágios Geórgios South ☕🌊🌳

( 13 km/8 mi )

⑲ Lefkími ☕

**Perivóli and head to the coast by taking the road in Perivóli to Kalivótis.** Your route now usually takes you **back north directly along the sea.** It is worth taking a coffee break at Nótos Beach in the **Panórama** taverna garden near **⑳ Petríti** → p. 78. At the fishing port in Petríti, the **narrow coastal road takes you past Búkari** with its many good fish tavernas to the two connected villages of **㉑ Messongí-Moraítika** → p. 75 where you can also eat well. It takes just 30 minutes by car back **to the island's capital ❶ Kérkyra** where your tour will end around 10pm.

| 19 km/12 mi |
| ⑳ Petríti |
| 8 km/5 mi |
| ㉑ Messongí-Moraítika |
| 20 km/12.5 mi |
| ❶ Kérkyra |

---

# ② ANCIENT KÉRKYRA – A WALKING TOUR OUTSIDE THE OLD TOWN

| | |
|---|---|
| START: ❶ Football stadium in Kérkyra<br>END: ⑭ Anemómilos windmill | 3–4 hours<br>Walking time<br>(without stops)<br>1.5 hours |
| Distance:<br>➡ 6 km/3.7 miles | |

COSTS: ❾ Mon Repos: admission 3 euros
WHAT TO PACK: mineral water, swimwear, picnic

IMPORTANT TIPS: city bus 15 takes you to the stadium, city buses 2a and 15 from Anemómilos take you back to the city centre. There is a bus stop at the park entrance of Mon Repos

On this stroll you will remain within the boundaries of the island's capital but will experience its rural side away from traffic. It not only offers beautiful natural scenery but also historical treats and will take you to two monasteries as well as a lush green bay for swimming. You will discover where the British Prince Philip was born and where the German Emperor Wilhelm II liked to take his archaeological spade in his hand. There is also time for a picnic in the old park next to the ancient columns.

**10:00am** The walk starts at the **❶ Football stadium in Kérkyra** in close proximity to the airport. **Starting out from the eastern side of the stadium, the route takes you first of all to the city's main cemetery** with its **❷ cemetery church**, which contains three valuable icons. **A very narrow tarmac lane leads you out of the cemetery** and after 80 m/262 ft, you will see the only remains of the ancient **❸ city wall of Kérkyra**. 17 stone layers from the 15th century have remained as they were used in the new construction of a basilica in early Chris-

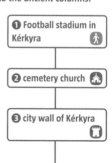

| ❶ Football stadium in Kérkyra |
| ❷ cemetery church |
| ❸ city wall of Kérkyra |

One of the highlights of this stroll is the small Classicist castle Mon Repos

④ Artemis Temple 🏛️

⑤ Ágii Theodóri 🏠

🌳

⑥ Paleópolis Basilica 🏠🌳

⑦ Roman thermal baths 🏛️

⑧ castle park of Mon Repos 🌳❄️

tian times. **Follow the lane further** past some plain farmhouses. Sheep graze, chickens peck and dogs laze about in the sunshine. A few minutes later you will come across the scanty remains of the ancient ④ **Temple**, Germany's Emperor Wilhelm II was especially interested in its excavation. It is right in front of the walls of the ⑤ **Ágii Theodóri convent**. One of the nuns who lives there will be pleased to show you around the convent church.

Stay on the small lane and **turn right onto the main road,** go past the agricultural research institute for olive cultivation and a primary school in traditional Classicist architecture and you will find yourself in front of the almost hidden entrance to the Mon Repos castle park. Here you can admire the view of the romantic, old walls from the wonderful, green area surrounding the ⑥ **Paleópolis Basilica** → p. 40 and see the excavations underneath a modern tent roof where ⑦ **Roman thermal baths** have been excavated. Now enter the ⑧ **castle park of Mon Repos** → p. 39. Start off by vis-

iting the small castle **⑨ Mon Repos**, where Philip, the husband of Queen Elizabeth II, was born on June 10, 1921 as a Greek Prince. Then follow the signs to the **Doric Temple**. **At the first junction, take a left along the shady path through the woods down to a small ⑩** INSIDER TIP **bathing bay** completely enclosed by trees with a jetty where you can take a quick dip. This is probably where Empress Sisi and family members of the German Emperor went swimming.

**12:00pm** The **main path** will take you past what is left of a **Hera Temple** to the extremely romantic foundations of the Doric **⑪ Kardáki Temple** adating back to the 5th century B.C. Some of its columns have been re-erected amidst the greenery and make a good photo opportunity. Very few visitors come here and there is no attendant so feel free to pack out your INSIDER TIP **picnic** surrounded by ancient columns.

A **very narrow, in parts overgrown path starting at the south-east corner of the temple area** takes you to the low wall surrounding the castle park. If you climb over it and **keep right on the path along the wall** you will reach the tiny hamlet of **Análipsi**. Here, you can follow the tarmac path along the castle wall back to the entrance and **then follow the main road turning right.** You will pass the entrance to the **⑫ Agías Efthímias convent → p. 34** with its splendid court-

⑨ Mon Repos 🏛

⑩ bathing bay 🌳 🏖

⑪ Kardáki Temple 🏛 🏖

⑫ Agías Efthímias convent 🏠

**⑬ Mon Repos Lido** 🚻🏖

**⑭ Anemómilos windmill** ⓘ☕🌺

yard. Shortly afterwards, you will reach the **⑬ Mon Repos Lido → p. 45** – in fact the only beach in this part of the city – and the **⑭ Anemómilos windmill** with the **Café Nautilus**, where you can end your afternoon with a splendid view of the Old Fort of Corfu.

# 3 VILLAGES AND BEACHES AROUND THE PANTOKRÁTOR

🚙

| START: ① Kérkyra | 10–12 hours |
| END: ① Kérkyra | Driving time |
| | (without stops) |

Distance:
🕐 **115 km/71.5 miles**

3–4 hours

**WHAT TO PACK:** Sun protection and swimwear

**IMPORTANT TIPS:** You'll need strong nerves to tackle the narrow, bendy road at the start of this tour. Treat yourself afterwards to a traditional ginger lemonade in Sokráki.

A tarmac road leads you up to the 906 m/2972 ft high Pantokrátor. Old Venetian villages around the mountain invite you to stroll around. No-through roads lead off from the main road taking you to small hamlets and beautiful beaches. A castle in Kassiópi invites you to stroll around its grounds while in Ágios Stéfanos you are close to Albania. Good taverns can be found in virtually all of the coastal resorts, as well as one high in the mountains in an old, desolate village.

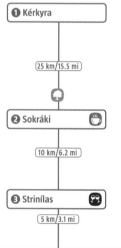

**① Kérkyra**

(25 km/15.5 mi)

**② Sokráki** ☕

(10 km/6.2 mi)

**③ Strinílas** 🍴

(5 km/3.1 mi)

**09:00am** From the town of ① **Kérkyra → p. 32** take the national road **in the direction of Paleokastrítsa before following the signs to the large mountain village of Áno Korakiána → p. 84** with its beautiful old houses. Then **follow the signs to Sokráki and Zigós.** The road now becomes narrower and winds like a corkscrew up the steep slope.

When you arrive in ② **Sokráki → p. 85** with its narrow road through the town, you might need to stop for a coffee or a glass of the typical Corfiot lemonade called *tzizimbírra.* Then **drive downhill slightly** to then start your ascent of the Pantokrátor. Let yourself be tempted to take a break in the village of ③ **Strinílas → p. 56** at the **Taverna Oasis** under a more than 200-year-old elm tree on the village square. The entire island of Corfu lies spread out be-

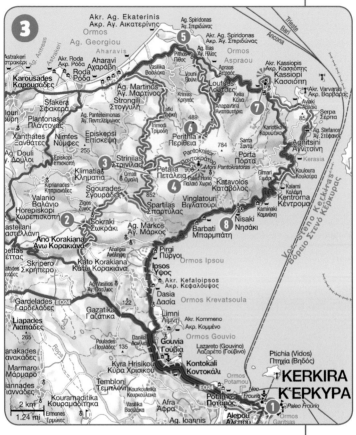

neath you when you reach the summit of **④ Pantokrátor** → p. 54.

**01:00pm** Back on the main road, return to Petalia and then **head north to the coast** until you reach Acharavi → p. 48 and **there take a right to bring you to your next destination: ⑤ Ágios Spirídonas** → p. 51. where you can choose to go for a swim and have something to eat. But you might prefer to have lunch in the next village on your tour: the old Venetian settlement of **⑥ Paleó Períthia** → p. 54 in a high valley at the foot of the Pantokrátor **where you then take the small road at Perouli back inland.** After a stroll through the ghost

**④ Pantokrátor**

21 km / 13 mi

**⑤ Ágios Spirídonas**

10 m / 33 ft

**⑥ Paleó Períthia**

The bays near Kassiópi are small but the translucent water is a delight for snorkelers

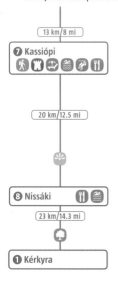

13 km/8 mi

**❼ Kassiópi**

20 km/12.5 mi

**❽ Nissáki**

23 km/14.3 mi

**❶ Kérkyra**

village of Paleó Períthia, **carry on back to the coast to** ❼ **Kassiópi** → p. 58. The best way to soak in the beauty of this place is to take the 25-minute walk around the peninsula with its **castle** → p. 58. On the way you will pass **Batería Beach** with its INSIDER TIP splendid spot for bathing and snorkelling as well as a good tavern.

Drive back **to the south along the coastal road. Ágios Stéfanos Siniés** → p. 61, close to Albania, **Kulúra** → p. 62 with its circular harbour and **Kalámi** → p. 62 are well worth a look and offer a good photo opportunity. However you should definitely drive down to the old port in ❽ **Nissáki** and let the day come to a close on the terrace of the **Mítsos** taverna near the sea or go to the tiny beach for a last dip. The road around the island then becomes less bendy and **you'll be back in** ❶ **Kérkyra in about half an hour.**

# 4

## SHOPPING IN CORFU STYLE BETWEEN GUVIÁ AND PALEOKASTRÍTSA

**START:** ❶ Guviá, at the traffic light crossroads
**END:** ❼ Paleokastrítsa

**Distance:**
➡ 15 km/9.3 miles

2–6 hours
Driving time
(without stops)
30 minutes

**COSTS:** Aquarium with boat trip costs 12.50 euros
**WHAT TO PACK:** enough cash, swimwear

**IMPORTANT TIPS:** No payment with credit card possible.

The shops along the main road from Guviá to Paleokastrítsa will invite you to head inland and tempt you to buy some souvenirs or look over the shoulders of the craftsmen at work. In stark contrast to end this tour: a monastery, aquarium with boat trip and a refreshing dip in the sea.

**10:00am** Soon after **turning off the road around the island at** ❶ Guviá → p. 86 you can first stock up with delicious baked Corfiot pastries at the popular ❷ **Emeral Bakery** on the left. There is an enormous selection of freshly baked goods and extremely affordable coffee here. Then continue and **on the right-hand side** you will see Sofoklís Ikonomídis and Sissy Moskídu's ❸ **Ceramic Workshop**

❶ Guviá
[ 1.5 km/1 mi ]

❷ Emeral Bakery
[ 2 km/1.25 mi ]
❸ Ceramic Workshop

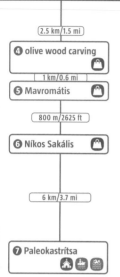

4 olive wood carving

2.5 km/1.5 mi

5 Mavromátis

1 km/0.6 mi

6 Níkos Sakális

800 m/2625 ft

6 km/3.7 mi

7 Paleokastrítsa

where they create, fire and paint colourful ceramic objects on the premises. After another few minutes in the car, visit the 4 **olive wood carving** exhibition **on the left of the road.** Shortly afterwards, you will reach the 5 **Mavromátis** Distillery **on the right** where the company's liqueurs can be purchased in the modern, air-conditioned showroom.

**600 m/1968 ft further on, a no-through-road off to the left to the Hotel Fundána** will lead you past a traditionally painted country house. This is where 6 INSIDER TIP **Níkos Sakális** produces and sells high-quality leather bags, glasses cases, backpacks and book covers (follow signs to the "Leather Workshop"). All of his products bear the "Seminole" trademark. The visit to the leather workshop ends our shopping tour. Perhaps now you're ready for a relaxing swim, or just enjoy the countryside or a bit of culture. You can have all of these things **after a ten-minute drive to the coast, to** 7 **Paleokastrítsa → p. 63.** First visit the **monastery,** then the **Corfu Aquarium → p. 116.** Follow with a trip on the **glass floor boat,** before taking a dip at the beach directly on the narrow stretch between the village and the monastery to complete your tour between 2pm–4pm.

A well-earned break after shopping in the green courtyard of the monastery in Paleokastrítsa

## 5 BOAT TRIP TO ALBANIA

**START:** ❶ Kérkyra ferry harbour
**END:** ❶ Kérkyra ferry harbour

1 day
Driving time in Albania
(without stops)
approx. 50 min.

Distance:
🔁 Ferry 30 km/18 miles, taxi 40 km/25 miles

**COSTS:** Return boat ticket 38 euros (mid June–mid Sept. costs 47.60 euros), taxi journey in Albania costs approx. 50 euros/taxi
❹ Butrint: admission approx. 6 euros
**WHAT TO PACK:** passport, small change and small euro notes as well as swimwear, walking boots, picnic, rain jacket, sun protection, water

**IMPORTANT TIPS:** Albania is one hour ahead of Corfu all year round. Journey by ferry or by hydrofoil takes approx. 30 min, motorised ship takes approx. 75 min. Timetables available at www.ionian-cruises.com, more information: www.visitsaranda.com

Corfu's northeast coast doesn't face Greece, but Albania. Until 1990, this neighbouring country was completely cut off from Corfu and the rest of the world, but now ferries and hydrofoils travel daily to the Albanian harbour town of Saranda. It is easy to enter the country and the euro is accepted everywhere. This excursion will take you to a country where almost nobody spends their holidays and you can take a taxi to visit the most magnificent archaeological sites far and wide.

**❶ Kérkyra ferry harbour**

`30 km/18.5 mi`

**❷ Saranda**

`20 km/12.5 mi`

**❸ Vivar Channel**

`200 m/218 yd`

**❹ Butrint**

**❺**

SHQIPËRIA  Finiq

Sarandë

Mesopotam

`78`

`99`

Çaush

Lekurës

`97`

`98`

Kassiópi

Liqen i Butrintit

Pantokrátor

●906

**❺** Butrint `825`

**❸** **❹**

Nissáki

Parku Kombëtar i Butrintit

Çiflik

Vório Stenó

Kérkiras

**Kérkira**

Κέρκυρα

**❶**

✈

CFU

Gastoúri

576 ★Ahélion

5 km

3.12 mi

**09:00am** Depending on the ferry, the crossing from **❶ Kérkyra ferry harbour** takes 30–75 minutes **to the port in Albania located at the small coastal town of ❷ Saranda**, which the Greeks call Ágíi Saránda. Although it only has 35,000 inhabitants, the many new eight-to-ten-storey buildings give it the appearance of being much larger. However there is no life in many of the apartments; Albanians working abroad have bought them as an investment and are seldom here.

Taxis are waiting immediately after the passport control at the **ferry harbour** that you can hire for approximately two hours to take you to the excavations at Butrint. **The road takes you across the narrow strip of land between the sea and Lake Butrint** to the **❸ Vivar Channel** that connects the lake with the sea. The entrance to the excavation site of the ancient **❹ Butrint** *(daily 9am–6pm)* is extremely close to the channel. The mountains you can see across the water are on mainland Greece.

The city of Butrint was founded around 1200 B.C. and was inhabited for more than 2,800 years until well into the 16th century. It experienced its golden age in the Roman period and most of its – often well preserved – historical monuments date back to this period. Today ancient Butrint is listed as a Unesco World Heritage Site. The **excavation site** is on a peninsula jutting into Lake Butrint that rises up to a height of 30 metres. It is densely wooded and the 50-minute walk seems like a stroll through a park. There are

Remnants of Albania's grand past: ancient Butrint

boards with detailed information in English, ground plans and sketches of the reconstruction of everything that can be seen here: **Roman baths** and a **Roman theatre**, the baptistery of an early-Christian **basilica** that has been preserved up as far as roof level, the partially very well preserved **city walls** and several **city gates** from various periods. After visiting the excavation site, you can enjoy a coffee in the **Hotel Butrint** in its pretty garden. **On your return to Saranda,** your taxi driver will be happy to show you the pretty beaches of ❺ **Ksamil** with a view of the off-shore islets.

**01:00pm** In ❻ **Saranda** let the taxi driver drop you off at the marina where you can enjoy an affordable meal in an attractive setting at the INSIDERTIP **Limani** restaurant at the seaside. Then turn left at the Hotel Porto Eda and head into the city, taking another left at the first crossroads. You will soon reach the town's main square with its small green area and the remnants of the early Christian **Agía Saránda** basilica dating back to the 6th century behind the fences. Head back to the ferry harbour where the motorised ships and hydrofoils head back to the ❶ **Kérkyra ferry harbour** which will take around 10 minutes on foot.

6 km / 3.7 mi

❺ Ksamil

11 km / 6.8 mi

❻ Saranda

30 km / 18.6 mi

❶ Kérkyra ferry harbour

# SPORTS & ACTIVITIES

**Corfu is not a training camp for high-performance athletes. The island takes a slower pace in terms of the sporting activities available whether on, above and under water, on horseback, on foot or on a mountain bike saddle.**

Yoga and meditative courses are also available for those who prefer to slow things right down on holiday. But if you feel the need for more speed, you can take the helm of your own boat with up to 30 HP without even having a sailing licence.

## CRUISES

You can take a short cruise lasting one or several days around Corfu on a variety of boats. *Corfu Yachting (tel. 26 61 09 94 70 | www.corfuyachting.com)* in the marina at Guviá offers the greatest range of tours.

A one-day cruise on a wooden schooner from 1960 costs 100 euros per person, and 80 euros on a sailing catamaran. Glass-bottomed boats and traditional *káikis* are also available. If you want real luxury, you can hire a sleek motor yacht – complete with captain – for six people for a hefty 3950 euros for 24 hours (drinks included).

After just a few brief explanations, you can set off on your rented motorboat with up to 30 HP without even having a licence. The hire company will tell you exactly where you are allowed to go. All boats are equipped with life jackets and a two-way radio. There are boat hire companies with the usual facilities in many resorts on the

**Whether for the masses or the selected few, Corfu offers a great variety of sports – ranging from free-of-charge to fiendishly expensive**

east and north coasts, as well as on the small neighbouring island of Páxos.

## DIVING

Around Corfu you'll find a rich submarine life. There are very few restrictions on diving, making the area ideal for this sport. The best diving grounds are on the coast between Paleokastrítsa and Érmones. As this rocky area can only be reached from the land side at a few places, most of the dives start from boats. All diving centres on Corfu give individual instruction and organise dives for tourists. All diving centres on Corfu offer lessons for beginners, special courses and one-to-one scuba diving instruction for individual divers. Absolute beginners can join in introductory diving courses (44 euros) and snorkelling tours (30 euros). ● *Korfu Diving (Paleokastrítsa | Ambeláki Bay | tel. 26 6304 16 04 | www.korfudiving.com)* and *Corfu Dive Club (Liápades | Hotel Blue Princess | mobile tel. 69 77 59 75 88 | www. corfudiveclub.com).*

## GOLF

Corfu has the greenest and most-cared-for 18-hole golf course in Greece. The high trees and small ponds give the course in the Ropa Valley its special atmosphere; the clubhouse with its restaurant and small pro-shop is another plus. Guests are welcome. *Corfu Golf Club (tel. 26 61 09 42 20; in winter, tel. 2106 92 30 29 | www.corfugolfclub.com)*

## HIKING

With its many shady paths, green valleys and countless villages, Corfu is an ideal hiking region. You can never get completely lost because there is almost always a village in sight. The loveliest hikes run from south to north on the 222 km (138 miles) long, unfortunately not well-marked, INSIDER TIP *Corfu Trail* that goes from Cape Akotíri Arkoúdia to Cape Akotíri Ágias Ekaterínis. More information and links to hike organisers along this long-distance path: *www.thecorfutrail.com*

## HORSE RIDING

The best-run riding stable on the island offers tours for beginners and experts: INSIDER TIP *Trailriders (Mon–Sat 10am–noon and 5–7pm | free transfers in the region between Paleokastrítsa and Gouviá | near Áno Korakiána, signposted from there | tel. 69 46 65 33 17 | www.trailriderscorfu.com).*

## MOUNTAINBIKING

Three companies offer INSIDER TIP guided mountainbike tours with various levels of difficulty. They, and some other smaller firms, also have bikes for hire (from 13 euros/day). Guided day tours start at 32 euros (10 % internet discount). Fly-&-Bike-programs: *The Corfu Mountainbike Shop (Dassiá | on the main road | tel. 26 61 09 33 44 | www.mountainbikecorfu.gr); S-A-F Travel/Hellas Bike (Skombú | on the Guviá-Paleokastrítsa road | tel. 26 61 09 75 58 | mobile tel. 69 45 52 80 31); S-Bikes (on the main road | Acharávi | tel. 26 63 06 41 15 | www.corfumountainbikes.com); Ionian Bike (Ágios Ioánnis | mobile tel. 69 09 75 98 17 | www.ionianbike-hike.nl).*

## TENNIS

Most of the large hotels have tennis courts; some are also available to people not staying in the hotel. The best complex that is open all year round and very popular with Corfiots has seven floodlit courts under the shade of pine trees: *Daphníla Tennis Club (near Grecotel Daphníla Bay in Daphníla | tel. 26 61 09 05 70).*

## WATERSPORTS & YACHTING

There are water sports centres at all of the main hotels and popular beaches. The bays between Dassiá and Kontokáli are particularly suited to waterskiing: a round costs about 25–30 euros. Here, there are also many kinds of fun rides (banana-ride, 15 euros/ride). Paragliding is also available on many beaches but there are great price differences depending on the season and centre. A solo glider pays between 45 and 50 euros; tandems, from 60 to 70 euros.

Windsurfers, dinghy and catamaran sailors are drawn to the west coast where the winds are stronger. There are good centres in Paleokastrítsa, Ágios Geórgios Pagón and Érmones. Kite-surfing is only possible in Ágios

Geórgios Argirádon. SUPs are available for hire, and guided Stand-Up-Paddling tours are also organised: *www.kite-club-corfu.com*.

Those with a license for open-sea sailing can rent yachts by the week – some with a skipper. *Corfu Yachting (Marina Guviá | tel. 26 61 09 94 70 | www.corfuyachting.com); Tsigorítis Maritime Holidays (Marina Guviá | tel. 26 61 09 18 88 | tsiri gotis.com).*

## WELLBEING & YOGA

The range of spa facilities on offer on Corfu is rather mediocre with only a few of the larger hotels having these. If a massage in the middle of an old village could tempt you, head to *Torsten Tilmanns (mobile tel. 69 38 79 97 23 | www.corfu-physio.com)* in Afiónas. Beauty treatments are also offered at the Panórama tavern (see p. 79) in a small park on Nótos Beach. However, the island is first-rate if you are interested in far-eastern practices such as yoga and meditation and you will find many organisers based along the coast between Ágios Geórgios Pagón and Arillás (see p. 56).

Those looking for a challenge should follow the Corfu Trail across the entire island

# TRAVEL WITH KIDS

**Corfu is a problem-free destination for families with children. The little ones are welcome everywhere. The Greeks don't fuss about their children very much but simply let them take part in most adult activities – and let them stay up until well past midnight.**

You can choose from a wide range of baby food, nappies and fresh milk in the supermarkets. There are reductions for children up to the age of 12 on bus services, ships and excursion boats, as well as at various events, and most of the large hotels have paddling pools.

If you stay in a hotel or apartment without a pool, you will be welcome to use any hotel pool as long as you buy drinks and snacks at the bar.

However, some things could be better on Corfu: highchairs and special meals for children are rare and even car hire services hardly ever have child seats. There is a playground in almost every village but the equipment is usually in a poor state of repair. Despite this, there is often a lot going on here in the early evening when the sun has lost its strength and the stars start to emerge. There are no restrictions or fences to stop children playing in the ruins of Corfiot castles – but the pits and walls are also unsecured and not without their dangers.

A word about your first-aid kit: doctors often prescribe antibiotics to cure simple colds; if you don't approve of this, you should make sure you have your

The kids will have a great time – fun for the whole family in the water and on dry land

own selection of medicine with you.
The flat, wind-sheltered bays on the east coast are much better for children who cannot swim than the beaches on the west where the water quickly becomes deep and there is often a slight swell and strong undercurrents. The best beaches for children are in the wide bay at Lefkími and in Dassiá where the water is comparatively safe.

### CORFU TOWN

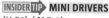 INSIDER TIP MINI DRIVERS
(U F4) (*D 5*)

On almost every summer evening between 6 and 10pm there is masses going on at the southern end of the Esplanade. This is where a child's dream comes true in the form of small electric cars that can be driven by anyone capable of holding a steering wheel and reaching the pedals – which sometimes proves easier than taking the foot off the accelerator. There is room in the cars for two children. It's a good idea to keep an eye on the little ones as there is no fence around the driving area: runaways can drive almost anywhere just as long as the battery holds out. Around 3 euros for 10 minutes of childhood bliss.

## MINI-TRAIN ON WHEELS
(U E4) (*m D 5*)

Miniature trains with a locomotive and three carriages with room for around 20 people in each are popular throughout Greece. They travel on rubber tyres and run on electric motors. The *trenáki* – Greek for little train – in Kérkyra makes 40-minute tours along the coast road to Paleópolis every hour between 10am and 2pm, and 5 and 8pm. The station is in front of Hotel Arcadíon on the Esplanade; the price is the same for everybody over the age of four: 6 euros.

## STARING PILOTS IN THE EYE
(135 E6) (*m D5*)

The airport runway in Corfu is at sea level. And ● *Kanóni,* the cape of Análipsis Peninsula, rises up only about 300 m/984 ft from its southern end as the crow flies. You can sit up there on a café terrace and have a fine view of the planes coming in to land or preparing to take off. If the planes land from the south, you will almost be able to look straight into the pilot's eye – you are both on the same level. It is just as fascinating to watch the planes turn at the southern end of the runway and see how they gain speed and then take off. Something else both young and old will enjoy up here: the refreshing sundaes are really a treat!

## TOURS WITH A HORSE AND CART
(U F4 and C1) (*m D 5*)

You will often hear the clatter of hooves in Kérkyra from one of the many one-horse carriages pulled by colourfully decorated horses in the Old Town. There is enough room in them for four adults (or two adults and four small children). But, you will have to dig deep into your pockets: 30 minutes cost about 30 euros (try to barter!). The carriages line up waiting for customers in front of the Schulenburg Monument on the Esplanade and, in the morning, at the Old Port. The best time to take a ride is in the early evening.

## THE NORTH

## CORFU AQUARIUM AND GLASS-BOTTOM BOAT
(134 B4) (*m B4*)

Mediterranean fish are exhibited in 19 separate pools. Even more exciting are the reptiles on display in an extra hall. After the aquarium, take a trip on the glass-bottom boat to see the fish in their natural habitat. *Daily 10am–6pm | admission 6 (children 4) euros, with boat trip 12.50 (children 6) euros | Paleokastrítsa | parking lot in front of the driveway to the monastery | www.corfuseadiscovery.com*

## CORFU DONKEY RESCUE
(134 C4) (*m B8*)

Who can seriously resist making the acquaintance of a friendly donkey? Set in a blanket of olive groves, the rescue sanctuary close to Paleokastrítsa welcomes visitors of all ages to come and stroke, feed and lead the donkeys (although you cannot ride the animals). This private animal rescue organisation has been committed to rescuing the grey furry animals from the Italian salami trade for many years. Visitors are also invited to make a Christmas donation to the sanctuary's account. You can also adopt a donkey for just 90 euros a year. *Daily 10am–5pm | admission free*

*| Liapádes | from Paleokastrítsa: approx. 2km/1.2mi after leaving the village behind the BP petrol station near Doukades. Take a left in the large left-hand bend in front of the Villa Alexandra and follow the signs | tel. 69 47 37 59 92 | www.corfu-donkey.com*

## HYDROPOLIS
(135 D1) (*ØJ C2*)

With its eight large water slides and numerous other facilities from water basketball to beach volleyball, tennis and billiard, this water park on the eastern edge of Acharávi is a real magnet. *May–Sept daily 10am–6pm | admission: adults 16 euros; children (5–12 years of age) 10 euros | www.gelinavillage.gr*

## CENTRAL CORFU

## AQUALAND
(135 D5) (*ØJ D5*)

The second of the two adventure water parks on Corfu, extending over an area of 75,000 m², is located near the village of Ágios Ioánnis in the verdant centre of the island. It has spacious lawns for sunbathing and its several freshwater pools, including some with wave machines, invite you to take a dip, while numerous giant slides make sure you hit the water with a splash.

There are self-service restaurants and bars and, if you like loud music all day long, just find a place near one of the loudspeakers. The number 8 bus leaves Kérkyra at 11am and 12:30, 2:15, 3:15 and 5pm and returns around 20 minutes later (tickets must be bought in advance at the kiosk). *May–Sept daily 10:30am–6:30pm | admission: adults 27 euros, children (5–12 years of age) and seniors 19 euros; weekly pass 70 euros | www.aqualand-corfu.com*

Asylum for donkeys in the privately run Corfu Donkey Rescue – a favourite attraction for children

# FESTIVALS & EVENTS

The Corfiot holiday calendar boasts many events that reveal Venetian and Orthodox influences. Here, the carnival is widely celebrated with many colourful balls, costume parties and parades. Holy Week and Easter closely follow the Orthodox tradition. The dates of these moveable feast days are different from other Christian churches. Church consecration festivals, which are celebrated in every village, form a symbiosis between the two. The Orthodox saints are lauded with music with an Italian touch on their feast day.

In Kérkyra in particular, there are numerous concerts and other cultural events throughout the summer season where you will be able to experience ancient tragedies and Greek rock music in open-air theatres and medieval castles.

## FESTIVALS & EVENTS

### 6 JANUARY
*Blessing of the Waters and Baptism of Christ:* Processions to the sea are held in all larger towns where a priest throws a cross into the waves. The young man who brings it back will be blessed by good fortune throughout the coming year.

### FEBRUARY/MARCH
Carnival processions in Kérkyra on the last three Sundays and Wednesday before Shrove Monday.

### SHROVE MONDAY
INSIDER TIP High-spirited atmosphere with music and dancing in Messongí.

### GOOD FRIDAY AND EASTER
Processions in all villages and in the capital, starting in the afternoon.
● Holy Saturday: Corfiots throw hundreds of clay jugs filled with water from balconies and windows onto the main streets in the Old Town. This turns into a public festival with music and sometimes dancing.
At 11pm, *Resurrection service* in all churches followed by fireworks
Easter Sunday: grilled lamb in every village; traditional *family festival*.

### MAY
20 and 21 May: *Church Consecration Festival* in honour of Saints Constantine and Helena in Nímfes.

### JUNE
Folklore dances in the theatre on several evenings at the end of the school year.

Something is always happening on the island – from the elaborate carnival celebrations to the church festivals in autumn

**EARLY JUNE–MID AUGUST**

During the ● *International Festival of Corfu*, there are about 20 evenings filled with lots of different concerts – from rock to classical, from choral music to piano recitals – in historical locations such as the Old Fort, St George's Church and the University's Ionian Academy. Admission is usually free.

**MID JULY**

16/17 July: *Church Consecration Festival* in Benítses with music, dancing and small gifts for visitors
Three-day *Cultural Festival* with plays and concerts in Gardíki Fortress on the second-to-last weekend in July.

**AUGUST**

10 August: Live music, boat processions and folklore during the *Barcarolle Festival* in the suburb of Garítsa
14/15 August: *Church Consecration Festivals* with music and dancing in Kassiópi and Paleokastrítsa and on 23/24 Aug in Ágii Déka and Pélekas.

## NATIONAL HOLIDAYS

| | |
|---|---|
| 1 January | New Year's Day |
| 6 January | Epiphany |
| 19 Feb 2018, 11 March 2019 | |
| | Shrove Monday |
| 25 March | National Holiday |
| 6 April 2018, 26 April 2019 | |
| | Good Friday |
| 8/9 April 2018, 28/29 April 2019 | |
| | Easter |
| 1 May | Labour Day |
| 21 May | Union of the Ionian Islands with Greece |
| 27/28 May 2018, 16/17 June 2019 | |
| | Whitsun |
| 15 August | Assumption of Mary |
| 28 October | National Holiday |
| 25/26 Dec | Christmas |

# LINKS, BLOGS, APPS & MORE

www.greencorfu.com Website on nature and"'green" affairs on the island. The accompanying blog.greencorfu.com gives lots of information about local products, alternative forms of tourism and environmental awareness as well as a lot of other tips and advice for the ecologically minded

www.allcorfu.com Comprehensive commercial website on all places on Corfu

www.corfu-kerkyra.eu/html/english/index.htm All of Corfu at a glance: the best beaches, resorts and restaurants, as well as a short Greek dictionary

www.agni.gr Website in English of a taverna and travel agency in north-eastern Corfu; also, general information and a unique selection of – sometimes unusual – holiday homes; for example, an old olive mill or an ancient house on the harbour pier in Lóngos on the neighbouring island of Páxos

www.corfu.gr With a mass on information on the island's history, climate and environment issues as well as what to do and where to eat

corfubloggers.blogspot.com English blog by four women – three British and one Dutch – who have lived on Corfu for years and provide the latest news update

twitter.com/GayCorfu This twitter blog of the private gaycorfuinfo.com portal gives news and information on gay events in summer

Regardless of whether you are still preparing your trip or already in Corfu: these addresses will provide you with more information, videos and networks to make your holiday even more enjoyable.

www.facebook.com/pages/corfu-paragliding/ 79007569977 Tips of all sorts are posted on the Corfu Paragliding Community pinboard and the latest information exchanged among sports freaks. Members also have fun posting their latest aerial pictures

www.corfuvisit.net The official site of the Corfu Town Council also presents videos including a 22-minute film about the island

www.greeka.com Many videos including a 10-minute, 16 mm one about the island that was filmed in 1972

www.corfu-tube.com If you manage to separate the grain from the chaff, you will find interesting videos made by visitors for visitors

www.youtube.com/watch?v=XVA-9fUiNeM Corfu from above: As an EasyJet flight approaches Corfu airport, there are beautiful views of the south of the island

www.youtube.com/watch?v=poZRlwLX2Tk Two men set out to walk on the Corfu Trail. This is their filmed diary

Walk Corfu Free English-language app to help you find your way on the Corfu Trail

Greece Radio Recorder Free app with which you can listen to numerous Greek radio stations streamed live

iSlands Island hopping and excursion planning become easier with this app. Available in Greek and English

Corfuguide The integrated map in this android app helps you find sights, hotels, restaurants and petrol stations. A calendar shows current events, and ferry connections make island hopping easy

# TRAVEL TIPS

## ARRIVAL

✈ Many airlines fly to Corfu in summer and there are flights via Athens throughout the year. The flight from London takes around 3¼ hours. Corfu's airport is on the outskirts of the town. You can easily take a taxi to your hotel or the coach terminal in Kérkyra. There are huge differences in the prices of flights and sometimes scheduled flights via Athens are cheaper than charters. The following sites can be recommended for more information: *en.aegeanair.com*, *www.aua.com*, *www.easyjet.com*, *www.olympicair.com*, *www.ryanair.com*

⛴ In the summer months, there are several daily connections with the Italian ports of Ancona, Bari, Brindisi and Venice. Depending on the ship, the crossing to Brindisi takes from 3½–8 hours; to Ancona, around 20; and 29–36 hours to Venice. Compare prices at *www.gtp.gr*, *www.greekferries.gr*, *www.minoan.gr*, *www.superfast.com* or contact a travel agent.

🚂🚌 Travelling by bus or train to an Italian harbour is only advisable in exceptional cases. Information on timetables and schedules is available at *www.raileurope-world.com* and *www.eurolines.de/en/home*.

## BUSES

Urban public buses are *the* mode of public transport on Corfu. You must purchase tickets in advance from kiosks, ticket machines or in your hotel. Bus number 2 takes you to the ferry port, Mon Repos and Kanóni, number 7 to Dassiá, number 5 to Kinopiástes, number 6 to Benítses, number 8 to Ágios Ioánnis, number 10 to Achíllio, number 11 to Pélekas. Line 15 connects the airport to the coach terminal, city centre and new ferry port. Bus number 16 connects the old port to the cruise ship terminal if cruise ships are docked in the port. If possible, you should buy your tickets for long-distance buses/coaches at the bus station – if not, when you get on the bus. Timetables for city buses can be found at *www.astikoktelkerkyras.gr*, for coaches at *www.greenbuses.gr*

## CAMPING

Camping anywhere else but in a camp site is forbidden on Corfu. There are eight official camp sites on the island – those in Dassiá, Káto Korakiána and Róda have a pool – but are only open in the summer season.

## RESPONSIBLE TRAVEL

It doesn't take a lot to be environmentally friendly whilst travelling. Don't just think about your carbon footprint whilst flying to and from your holiday destination but also about how you can protect nature and culture abroad. As a tourist it is especially important to respect nature, look out for local products, cycle instead of driving, save water and much more. If you would like to find out more about eco-tourism please visit: *www.ecotourism.org*

# From arrival to weather

## CAR HIRE

Bicycles, mopeds, motor scooters, motorbikes, 4x4s and cars can be rented in all of the holiday resorts on Corfu. A Vauxhall Corsa costs from around 35 euros per day. If you want to hire a car or motorbike, you have to be at least 23 years of age. Be careful: even if you have full insurance coverage, damage to the tyres and the underside of the car is not covered. No matter how small the accident, you should call the police – otherwise, the insurance company will not pay. And, if you rent a moped, it is a good idea to wear jeans even if the weather is hot; they will provide increased protection if you have a slight accident and fall.

There is a good network of filling stations on the island and all sell both petrol and diesel. Most garages are open daily from 8am to 8pm. Self-service is still uncommon and coin-operated petrol stations are rare. Fuel prices are considerably higher than in many other countries in Europe.

The speed limit in built-up areas is 50 km/h and 90 km/h on main roads. It is compulsory to wear seatbelts in the front seats. The blood alcohol limit is 0.5; 0.2 for motorbike riders. The fines for traffic offences are extremely high. The police usually demand 60 euros for illegal parking that must be paid to the authority stated on the ticket.

## CLIMATE, WHEN TO GO

The high season on Corfu lasts from May to October. Many hotels and most of the restaurants outside of the island's capital are closed in the other months. In May, the sea can still be too cold for swimming but this is the month when the flowers are at their best. The water is pleasantly warm in autumn but by this time the vegetation is largely withered and burnt. It hardly rains between June and September but there are often very strong winds.

The capital, Kérkyra, is also an attractive winter destination. There are almost no holidaymakers during this period and the locals have time to enjoy themselves in the tavernas. There will be fires blazing in the open hearths in the bars, restaurants and cafés – and you will have the museums all to yourself!

## BUDGETING

| | | |
|---|---|---|
| Bus | 0.20 euros | per kilometre in the country |
| Coffee | 2.50 euros | for a cup of coffee |
| Pedal boat | 10 euros | for an hour |
| Wine | 3.50 euros | for a glass |
| Snack | 2.30 euros | for gyros at a stand |
| Petrol | 1.60 euros | for 1 litre of super |

## CONSULATES AND EMBASSIES

### BRITISH VICE CONSULATE

*18 Mantzarou Street 491 00, Kérkyra | tel.: 266 10-300 55 / 234 57 | fax: 266 10-379 95 | www.gov.uk/world/organisations/british-vice-consulate-corfu | Email: Corfu@fco.gov.uk*

**U.S. EMBASSY (ATHENS)**
*91 Vasilisis Sophias Avenue | 10160 Athens | tel.: 2107212951 | gr.usembassy. gov/embassy-consulate/athens*

## EMERGENCY SERVICES

112 for the police, fire brigade and ambulance; 171 for the tourist police

## CUSTOMS

EU citizens can import and export goods for their personal use tax-free (800 cigarettes, 1 kg tobacco, 90 l of wine, 10 l of spirits over 22%). Visitors from other countries must observe the following limits, except for items for personal use. Duty free are: max. 50 g perfume, 200 cigarettes, 50 cigars, 250 g tobacco, 1 L of spirits (over 22% vol.), 2 L of spirits (under 22% vol.), 2 L of any wine. Gifts to the value of up to 430 euros may be brought into Greece. Special regulations for souvenirs from day trips to Albania: You may only bring back 40 cigarettes, 1 L of spirits or 2 L of wine.

## DISCOTHEQUES

Greek discos do not usually open before 10 or 11pm. There is generally no entrance fee but the drinks are expensive; a long drink costs between 6 and 10 euros, a small bottle of beer 3 to 5 euros. There is hardly an age check.

## ELECTRICITY

Corfu has the same 220 volt as most continental European countries. You will need an adapter if you want to use a UK plug.

## ENTRANCE FEES

A joint ticket for the Archaeological Museum, Museum for Asian Art, the Byzantine Museum and Old Fortress is available at the ticket desk of any one of the four institutions for 8 euros. This represents a saving of 4 euros compared to the price of separate tickets. National museums give discounts to pensioners over 65 years of age. Children from EU countries and students with an International Student Card are granted free admission. There is no entrance fee for visiting churches and monasteries but donations are always welcome. The most discreet way to do this is to buy candles and light them in front of an icon with an optional prayer of intercession.

# FOR BOOKWORMS AND FILM BUFFS

**Family and Other Animals** – Gerald Durrell's humorous and much-loved description of his experiences on Corfu where he spent his childhood in the 1930s

**Fedora** – Billy Wilder's bizarre story of a Hollywood star who also spent some time on Corfu; with Hildegard Knef and Mario Adorf in the main roles

**For Your Eyes Only** – The James Bond adventure story begins off the coast of Corfu and parts of it were shot on the island in 1980

**Prospero's Cell: A Guide to the Landscape and Manners of the Island of Corfu** – His even more famous brother Lawrence Durrell captured the feeling of this period in his works of literature

## HEALTH

Well-trained doctors guarantee basic medical care. However, there is often a lack of medical equipment. The standard of the government hospital in Kérkyra is low. Complicated cases are sent to Athens. If you are seriously ill or injured, you should try to fly home. Emergency treatment in hospitals and government health centres *(ESY, National Health Centre)* is free of charge. Theoretically, medical treatment from doctors in the state scheme is also free if you present the European Health Insurance Card issued by your own insurance company. However, in practice this is complicated and time-consuming. It is highly recommended that you take out an international health insurance; you can then choose your doctor, pay him in cash, get a receipt and then present your bills to the insurance company for refunding. Chemists are well-stocked but do not always have British medication. In Greece, many medicines which are only available if you have a prescription in other countries, can be purchased without one and are cheaper than at home – e.g. painkillers and remedies for heartburn and herpes. You are only able to import small quantities.

Mosquitoes also like Corfu. You should have mosquito protection in your first-aid kit as well as something for insect bites. Bathing shoes will protect you from sea urchins. There are no poisonous snakes or scorpions on the island.

## HOLIDAY RENTALS

The following websites specialise in holiday properties and apartments on Corfu:
– *http://corfuvillaowners.com*
– *http://www.corfu-holiday-rentals.co.uk*
– *www.kassiopi.com*

## IMMIGRATION INTO GREECE

A valid passport is required for entry into Greece. All children must travel with their own passport.

## INFORMATION

**GREEK NATIONAL TOURISM ORGANISATION**
– *5th Floor East, Great Portland House | 4 Great Portland Street | London, W1W 8QJ | tel. 020 7495 9300*
- *www.visitgreece.gr; www.corfuvisit.net*

## INTERNET & WIFI

Freshly laid strips of tarmac are visible along the roads in many Corfu villages. The reason is that fibre-optic cables have been installed all over Corfu. In keeping with the Greeks' understanding of democracy, free Wi-Fi is available almost everywhere on Corfu in tavernas, bars and simple *kafenía* – except in some luxury hotels. The password is usually the phone number or the sequence of digits 1 to 9 followed by a 0.

## LANGUAGE

The Greeks are proud of the characters in their language which are unique to Greece. Although place names and labels are often also written in Roman letters, it is still useful to have some knowledge of the Greek alphabet – and you need to know how to stress the words correctly to be understood. The vowel with the accent is emphasised.

## MONEY & CREDIT CARDS

The national currency is the euro. You can withdraw money from many ATMs with your credit or debit card. Banks and post offices cash traveller's cheques. Credit cards (especially Visa and MasterCard) are accepted by many hotels and restaurants but only by a few petrol stations, tavernas and shops. Bank opening hours are *Mon–Thur 8am–2pm, Fri 8am–1:30pm*.

## NEWSPAPERS

Foreign newspapers can usually be bought on Corfu one day after they appear. The English language weekly *Athens News* and monthly *The Corfiot* are published locally. *Corfu Gazette* and *The Agiot* are two monthly electronic newsletters.

# CURRENCY CONVERTER

| £ | € | € | £ |
|---|---|---|---|
| 1 | 1.13 | 1 | 0.89 |
| 3 | 3.39 | 3 | 2.66 |
| 5 | 5.64 | 5 | 4.43 |
| 13 | 14.67 | 13 | 11.52 |
| 40 | 45.15 | 40 | 35.44 |
| 75 | 85 | 75 | 66 |
| 120 | 135 | 120 | 106 |
| 250 | 282 | 250 | 221 |
| 500 | 564 | 500 | 443 |

| $ | € | € | $ |
|---|---|---|---|
| 1 | 0.87 | 1 | 1.16 |
| 3 | 2.60 | 3 | 3.47 |
| 5 | 4.33 | 5 | 5.78 |
| 13 | 11.25 | 13 | 15.03 |
| 40 | 34.61 | 40 | 46.24 |
| 75 | 65 | 75 | 87 |
| 120 | 104 | 120 | 139 |
| 250 | 216 | 250 | 289 |
| 500 | 433 | 500 | 578 |

For current exchange rates see www.xe.com

## PHONE & MOBILE PHONE

With the exception of some emergency numbers, all Greek telephone numbers have ten digits. There are no area dialling codes. Greek mobile phone numbers always begin with "6".

Dialling codes: Greece 0030 followed by the telephone number. Code for Australia (0061), Canada (001), Ireland (00353), United Kingdom (0044), USA (001) followed by the area code without "0". Phone booths are usually out of order – the mobile phone (called *kinitó*) has taken over here too. Only buy a phone card for *statheró* from a kiosk once you have found a phone booth which is working. Mobile phone reception is generally good except in some valleys. If you are based in the north of Corfu, make sure you do not make calls over an Albanian provider. The Greek pre-paid cards are recommended for those who phone a lot. These cards are available from the numerous shops run by telecommunications companies such as Cosmote, Vodafone and Wind. The first time you buy a pre-paid Greek card, you will have to register by presenting your passport. Cards for reloading can also be purchased from many kiosks and supermarkets.

## PHOTOGRAPHY

Taking pictures of military areas is forbidden. In museums, there is often a fee if you want to film. You need permission and pay a fee to take photos using a tripod or flash. Photographing is frowned upon in churches.

## POST

There are post offices in Kérkyra and all major villages. It usually takes 3 to 7 days for post to reach other European destinations. The large post offices always have a small selection of, often unusual, stamps. Post offices are usually open from Mon to Fri from 7:30am to 3pm.

## SMOKING

Smoking is prohibited in all forms of public transport, in airport terminals, inside restaurants and tavernas, in offices and in the public areas of the hotels. However, these laws are only observed sporadically in restaurants and tavernas in the country.

## TAXI

There are plenty of taxis in Kérkyra. You can flag them down, get in at the taxi ranks or telephone for one. The prices are set by the government and are comparatively low (e.g. Airport–town centre 10–15 euros). But, make sure that the taxi driver uses tariff 1 within the city limits; tariff 2 only applies to cross-country trips! Outside the town, the taxis are officially called *agoraíon*. Their rates are the same as taxis but they do not have a meter. You pay a set price for a specific distance.

## TIME

Greece is two hours ahead of Greenwich Mean Time, seven hours ahead of US Eastern Time and seven hours behind Australian Eastern Time.

## TIPPING

Like most other places in Europe, but at least 50 cents. In restaurants, you leave the tip on the table when leaving.

# WEATHER ON CORFU

| | Jan | Feb | March | April | May | June | July | Aug | Sept | Oct | Nov | Dec |
|---|---|---|---|---|---|---|---|---|---|---|---|---|
| Daytime temperatures in °C/°F | 16/61 | 16/61 | 17/63 | 20/68 | 24/75 | 28/82 | 29/84 | 29/84 | 27/81 | 24/75 | 21/70 | 17/63 |
| Night time temperatures in °C/°F | 9/48 | 9/48 | 10/50 | 12/54 | 15/59 | 19/66 | 21/70 | 22/72 | 19/66 | 16/61 | 14/57 | 11/52 |
| Sunshine hours/day | 3 | 5 | 6 | 8 | 10 | 12 | 13 | 12 | 10 | 6 | 6 | 4 |
| Precipitation days/month | 12 | 7 | 8 | 4 | 2 | 1 | 0 | 0 | 2 | 6 | 6 | 10 |
| Water temperature in °C/°F | 16/61 | 15/59 | 16/61 | 16/61 | 19/66 | 22/72 | 24/75 | 25/77 | 24/75 | 23/73 | 20/68 | 17/63 |

# USEFUL PHRASES GREEK

## PRONUNCIATION

We have provided a simple pronunciation aid for the Greek words
(see middle column). Note the following:
- ' the following syllable is emphasised
- ð in Greek (shown as "dh" in middle column) is like "th" in "there"
- θ in Greek (shown as "th" in middle column) is like "th" in "think"
- Χ in Greek (shown as "ch" in middle column) is like a rough "h" or
  "ch" in Scottish "loch"

| | | | | | | | | | | |
|---|---|---|---|---|---|---|---|---|---|---|
| Α | α | a | Η | η | i | Ν | ν | n | Τ | τ | t |
| Β | β | v | Θ | θ | th | Ξ | ξ | ks, x | Υ | υ | i, y |
| Γ | γ | g, y | Ι | ι | i, y | Ο | ο | o | Φ | φ | f |
| Δ | δ | th | Κ | κ | k | Π | л | p | Χ | χ | ch |
| Ε | ε | e | Λ | λ | l | Ρ | ρ | r | Ψ | ψ | ps |
| Ζ | ζ | z | Μ | μ | m | Σ | σ, ς s, ss | | Ω | ώ | o |

### IN BRIEF

|  |  |  |
|---|---|---|
| Yes/No/Maybe | ne/'ochi/'issos | Ναι/ Όχι/Ίσως |
| Please/Thank you | paraka'lo/efcharis'to | Παρακαλώ/Ευχαριστώ |
| Sorry | sig'nomi | Συγνώμη |
| Excuse me | me sig'chorite | Με συγχωρείτε |
| May I...? | epi'treppete ...? | Επιτρέπεται…? |
| Pardon? | o'riste? | Ορίστε? |
| I would like to.../ | 'thelo.../ | Θέλω…/ |
| have you got...? | 'echete...? | Έχετε…? |
| How much is...? | 'posso 'kani...? | Πόσο κάνει…? |
| I (don't) like this | Af'to (dhen) mu a'ressi | Αυτό (δεν) μου αρέσει |
| good/bad | ka'llo/kak'ko | καλό/κακό |
| too much/much/little | 'para pol'li/pol'li/'ligo | πάρα πολύ/πολύ/λίγο |
| everything/nothing | ólla/'tipottal | όλα/τίποτα |
| Help!/Attention!/ | vo'ithia!/prosso'chi!/ | Βοήθεια!/Προσοχή!/ |
| Caution! | prosso'chi! | Προσοχή! |
| ambulance | astheno'forro | Ασθενοφόρο |
| police/ | astino'mia/ | Αστυνομία/ |
| fire brigade | pirosvesti'ki | Πυροσβεστική |
| ban/ | apa'gorefsi/ | Απαγόρευση/ |
| forbidden | apago'revete | απαγορεύεται |
| danger/dangerous | 'kindinoss/epi'kindinoss | Κίνδυνος/επικίνδυνος |

# Milás elliniká?

"Do you speak Greek?" This guide will help you to say the basic words and phrases in Greek.

## GREETINGS, FAREWELL

| | | |
|---|---|---|
| Good morning!/afternoon!/evening!/night! | kalli'mera/kalli'mera!/kalli'spera!/kalli'nichta! | Καλημέρα/Καλημέρα!/Καλησπέρα!/Καληνύχτα! |
| Hello!/goodbye! | 'ya (su/sass)!/a'dio!/ya (su/sass)! | Γεία (σου/σας)!/αντίο!/Γεία (σου/σας)! |
| Bye! | me 'lene... | Με λένε… |
| My name is... | poss sass 'lene? | Πως σας λένε? |

## DATE & TIME

| | | |
|---|---|---|
| Monday/Tuesday | dhef'tera/'triti | Δευτέρα/Τρίτη |
| Wednesday/Thursday | tet'tarti/'pempti | Τετάρτη/Πέμπτη |
| Friday/Saturday | paraske'vi/'savatto | Παρασκευή/Σάββατο |
| Sunday/weekday | kiria'ki/er'gassimi | Κυριακή/Εργάσιμη |
| today/tomorrow/yesterday | 'simera/'avrio/chtess | Σήμερα/Αύριο/Χτες |
| What time is it? | ti 'ora 'ine? | Τι ώρα είναι? |

## TRAVEL

| | | |
|---|---|---|
| open/closed | annik'ta/klis'to | Ανοικτό/Κλειστό |
| entrance/driveway | 'issodhos/'issodhos ochi'matonn | Είσοδος/Είσοδος οχημάτων |
| exit/exit | 'eksodhos/'Eksodos ochi'matonn | Έξοδος/Έξοδος οχημάτων |
| departure/departure/arrival | anna'chorissi/anna'chorissi/'afiksi | Αναχώρηση/Αναχώρηση/Άφιξη |
| toilets/restrooms / ladies/gentlemen | tual'lettes/gine'konn/an'dronn | Τουαλέτες/Γυναικών/Ανδρών |
| (no) drinking water | 'possimo ne'ro | Πόσιμο νερό |
| Where is...?/Where are...? | pu 'ine...?/pu 'ine...? | Πού είναι/Πού είναι...? |
| bus/taxi | leofo'rio/tak'si | Λεωφορείο/Ταξί |
| street map/map | 'chartis tis 'pollis/'chartis | Χάρτης της πόλης/Χάρτης |
| harbour | li'mani | Λιμάνι |
| airport | a-ero'drommio | Αεροδρόμιο |
| schedule/ticket | drommo'logio/issi'tirio | Δρομολόγιο/Εισιτήριο |
| I would like to rent... | 'thelo na nik'yasso... | Θέλω να νοικιάσω… |
| a car/a bicycle/a boat | 'enna afto'kinito/'enna po'dhilato/'mia 'varka | ένα αυτοκίνητο/ένα ποδήλατο/μία βάρκα |
| petrol/gas station | venzi'nadiko | Βενζινάδικο |
| petrol/gas / diesel | ven'zini/'diesel | Βενζίνη/Ντίζελ |

## FOOD & DRINK

| | | |
|---|---|---|
| Could you please book a table for tonight for four? | Klis'te mass parakal'lo 'enna tra'pezi ya a'popse ya 'tessera 'atoma | Κλείστε μας παρακαλώ ένα τραπέζι γιά απόψε γιά τέσσερα άτομα |
| The menu, please | tonn ka'taloggo parakal'lo | Τον κατάλογο παρακαλώ |
| Could I please have...? | tha 'ithella na 'echo...? | Θα ήθελα να έχο …? |
| with/without ice/ sparkling | me/cho'ris 'pago/ anthrakik'ko | με/χωρίς πάγο/ ανθρακικό |
| vegetarian/allergy | chorto'fagos/allerg'ia | Χορτοφάγος/Αλλεργία |
| May I have the bill, please? | 'thel'lo na pli'rosso parakal'lo | Θέλω να πληρώσω παρακαλώ |

## SHOPPING

| | | |
|---|---|---|
| Where can I find...? | pu tha vro...? | Που θα βρω…? |
| pharmacy/ chemist | farma'kio/ ka'tastima | Φαρμακείο/Κατάστημα καλλυντικών |
| bakery/market | 'furnos/ago'ra | Φούρνος/Αγορά |
| grocery | pandopo'lio | Παντοπωλείο |
| kiosk | pe'riptero | Περίπτερο |
| expensive/cheap/price | akri'vos/fti'nos/ti'mi | ακριβός/φτηνός/Τιμή |
| more/less | pio/li'gotere | πιό/λιγότερο |

## ACCOMMODATION

| | | |
|---|---|---|
| I have booked a room | 'kratissa 'enna do'matio | Κράτησα ένα δωμάτιο |
| Do you have any... left? | 'echete a'komma... | Έχετε ακόμα… |
| single room | mon'noklino | Μονόκλινο |
| double room | 'diklino | Δίκλινο |
| key | kli'dhi | Κλειδί |
| room card | ilektronni'ko kli'dhi | Ηλεκτρονικό κλειδί |

## HEALTH

| | | |
|---|---|---|
| doctor/dentist/ paediatrician | ya'tros/odhondoya'tros/ pe'dhiatros | Ιατρός/Οδοντογιατρός/ Παιδίατρος |
| hospital/ emergency clinic | nossoko'mio/ yatri'ko 'kentro | Νοσοκομείο/ Ιατρικό κέντρο |
| fever/pain | piret'tos/'ponnos | Πυρετός/Πόνος |
| diarrhoea/nausea | dhi'arria/ana'gula | Διάρροια/Αναγούλα |
| sunburn | ilia'ko 'engavma | Ηλιακό έγκαυμα |
| inflamed/ injured | molli'menno/ pligo'menno | μολυμένο /πληγωμένο |
| pain reliever/tablet | paf'siponna/'chapi | Παυσίπονο/Χάπι |

## POST, TELECOMMUNICATIONS & MEDIA

| | | |
|---|---|---|
| stamp/letter | gramma'tossimo/'gramma | Γραμματόσημο/Γράμμα |
| postcard | kartpos'tall | Καρτ-ποστάλ |
| I need a landline phone card | kri'azomme 'mia tile'karta ya dhi'mossio tilefoni'ko 'thalamo | Χρειάζομαι μία τηλεκάρτα για δημόσιο τηλεφωνικό θάλαμο |
| I'm looking for a prepaid card for my mobile | tha 'ithella 'mia 'karta ya to kinni'to mu | Θα ήθελα μία κάρτα για το κινητό μου |
| Where can I find internet access? | pu bor'ro na vro 'prosvassi sto índernett? | Που μπορώ να βρω πρόσβαση στο ίντερνετ? |
| socket/adapter/ charger | 'briza/an'dapporras/ fortis'tis | πρίζα/αντάπτορας/ φορτιστής |
| computer/battery/ rechargeable battery | ippologis'tis/batta'ria/ eppanaforti'zomenni batta'ria | Υπολογιστής/μπαταρία/ επαναφορτιζόμενη μπαταρία |
| internet connection/ wifi | 'sindhessi se as'sirmato 'dhitio/vaifai | Σύνδεση σε ασύρματο δίκτυο/WiFi |

## LEISURE, SPORTS & BEACH

| | | |
|---|---|---|
| beach | para'lia | Παραλία |
| sunshade/lounger | om'brella/ksap'plostra | Ομπρέλα/Ξαπλώστρα |

## NUMBERS

| | | |
|---|---|---|
| 0 | mi'dhen | μηδέν |
| 1 | 'enna | ένα |
| 2 | 'dhio | δύο |
| 3 | 'tria | τρία |
| 4 | 'tessera | τέσσερα |
| 5 | 'pende | πέντε |
| 6 | 'eksi | έξι |
| 7 | ef'ta | εφτά |
| 8 | och'to | οχτώ |
| 9 | e'nea | εννέα |
| 10 | 'dhekka | δέκα |
| 11 | 'endhekka | ένδεκα |
| 12 | 'dodhekka | δώδεκα |
| 20 | 'ikossi | είκοσι |
| 50 | pen'inda | πενήντα |
| 100 | eka'to | εκατό |
| 200 | dhia'kossia | διακόσια |
| 1000 | 'chilia | χίλια |
| 10000 | 'dhekka chil'iades | δέκα χιλιάδες |

# ROAD ATLAS

The green line indicates the Discovery Tour "Corfu at a glance"
The blue line indicates the other Discovery Tours

All tours are also marked on the pull-out map

Photo: The harbour at Ágios Stéfanos

# Exploring Corfu

The map on the back cover shows how the area has been sub-divided.

**Kerkira (Korfu)**
**Κέρκυρα (Κόρφου)**

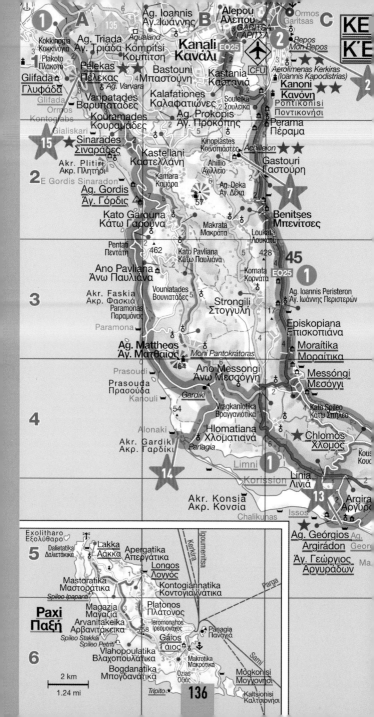

D  E  F

1  3  4

5  6

2 km
1.24 mi

**1**

Akr. Kalamas
Ακρ. Καλαμάς  **2**

Akr. Vatatsas
Ακρ. Βατάτσας

Ormos

Prasoudi
Πρασούδι  **3**

N o t i o   S t e n o   K e r k i r a s

Thiamis

Igoumenitsa

**4**

Korakades
Καρακάδες    Kolpos Lefkimis

Petriti ★
Πετρίτη

Akr. Lefkimis
Ακρ. Λευκίμης

Ag. Nikolaos
Αγ. Νικόλαος

Ag. Ioannis

Alikes
Αλυκές

1,5

Roumanades
Ρουμανάδες    Kaliviotis
Καλιβιώτης

Molos
Μόλος

Lefkimi
Λευκίμη

athias
αθείας

1,5

Perivoli
Περιβόλι

Ag. Taxiarhes

Ringlades
Ρίγγλαδες

3

3

Potami
Ποτάμι

**1**

**5**

53    EO25

Ano Lefkimi
Άνω Λευκίμη

4

Ag. Aikaterini

1  1,5

Melikia
Μελίκια

Lefkim

Ag. Varvara

28

1

vara
ara    Vitalades
Βιταλάδες

Ag. Anna

3

5,5

Βαρβάρα

Megahoros
Μεγάχωρος

Kritika
Κρητηκά

Neohori
Νεοχώρι

Kavos
Κάβος

Gardenos

Paleohori
Παλαιοχώρι

Ag. Markianos

Dragotina
Δραγοτίνα

Spartera
Σπαρτερά

Akr. Kountouris
Ακρ. Κούντούρης

**6**

Gaios

Ai Gordis Paleohoriou

2    134

Akr.
Ακρ.  **137**    dila
ίλα    Moni
Panagias

Akr. Asprohavos
Ακρ. Ασπρόχαβος

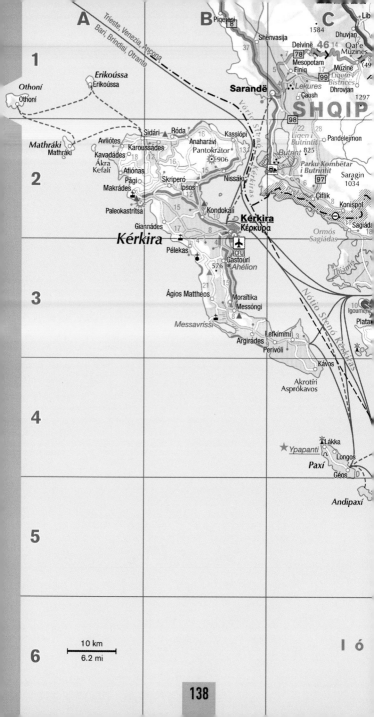

A  Trieste, Venezia, Ancona
Bari, Brindisi, Otranto

B  Piqeras 8  Lib

C  1584  Dhuvjan
Shënvasija  Delvinë 46 14  Qaf'e
37  78  Müzine  (49
Mesopotam  17  99
Finiq  Lrequres  Dhrovjan
Sarandë  Çaush  1297
Othoní  SHQIP
Othoní  98
Erikoússa  22  28
Erikoússa  Ligen i
Butrintit  Pandelejmon
Sidári  Róda  Kassiópi  Butrint 825
Mathráki  Avliótes  16  Anaharávi  13  Parku Kombëtar
Mathráki  Karoussádes  Pantokrátor  i Butrintit  Saragin
Kavadádes  18  12  906  Nissáki  97  1034
Ákra  Afiónas  16  15  6  Çiflik  8  Konispol
Kefalí  Pági  Skriperó  Ormós  Sagiáda
Makrádes  Ípsos  Kondokáli  Sagiádas  18
Paleokastrítsa  15  Kérkira  Thiamis
Giannádes  Κέρκυρα
Kérkira  17  8  Plata
Pélekas  4  CFU  10  Igoumeni
576  Gastoúri  Platą
Ágios Mattheos  Ahélion  Plata
21  Moraïtika
Messavríssi  Messóngi
8  Lefkímmi  3
Argirádes  Perivóli
Kávos
Akrotíri
Asprókavos
Ypapanti  Lákka
Paxí  Longos
Géos
Andipaxí

10 km
6.2 mi

Ió

138

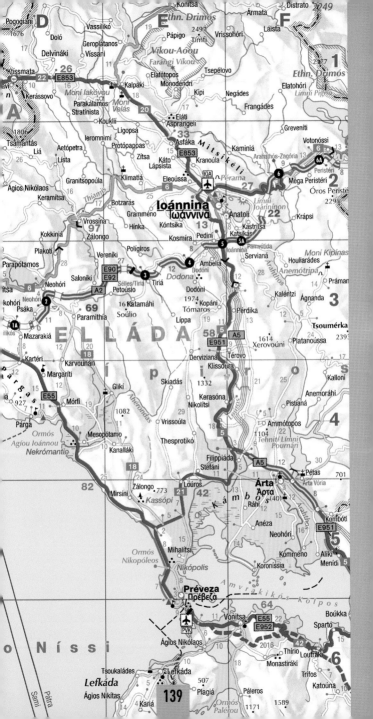

# KEY TO ROAD ATLAS

| | | |
|---|---|---|
| Autobahn · Gebührenpflichtige Anschlussstelle · Gebührenstelle · Anschlussstelle mit Nummer · Rasthaus mit Übernachtung · Raststätte · Kleinraststätte · Tankstelle · Parkplatz mit und ohne WC | | Motorway · Toll junction · Toll station · Junction with number · Motel · Restaurant · Snackbar · Filling-station · Parking place with and without WC |
| Autobahn in Bau und geplant mit Datum der voraussichtlichen Verkehrsübergabe | Datum  Date | Motorway under construction and projected with expected date of opening |
| Zweibahnige Straße (4-spurig) | | Dual carriageway (4 lanes) |
| Fernverkehrsstraße · Straßennummern | 14  E45 | Trunk road · Road numbers |
| Wichtige Hauptstraße | | Important main road |
| Hauptstraße · Tunnel · Brücke | )=( | Main road · Tunnel · Bridge |
| Nebenstraßen | | Minor roads |
| Fahrweg · Fußweg | | Track · Footpath |
| Wanderweg (Auswahl) | | Tourist footpath (selection) |
| Eisenbahn mit Fernverkehr | | Main line railway |
| Zahnradbahn, Standseilbahn | | Rack-railway, funicular |
| Kabinenschwebebahn · Sessellift | | Aerial cableway · Chair-lift |
| Autofähre · Personenfähre | | Car ferry · Passenger ferry |
| Schifffahrtslinie | | Shipping route |
| Naturschutzgebiet · Sperrgebiet | | Nature reserve · Prohibited area |
| Nationalpark · Naturpark · Wald | | National park · natural park · Forest |
| Straße für Kfz. gesperrt | X X X | Road closed to motor vehicles |
| Straße mit Gebühr | | Toll road |
| Straße mit Wintersperre | XII-II | Road closed in winter |
| Straße für Wohnanhänger gesperrt bzw. nicht empfehlenswert | | Road closed or not recommended for caravans |
| Touristenstraße · Pass | Weinstraße  1510 | Tourist route · Pass |
| Schöner Ausblick · Rundblick · Landschaftlich bes. schöne Strecke | | Scenic view · Panoramic view · Route with beautiful scenery |
| Heilbad · Schwimmbad | | Spa · Swimming pool |
| Jugendherberge · Campingplatz | | Youth hostel · Camping site |
| Golfplatz · Sprungschanze | | Golf-course · Ski jump |
| Kirche im Ort, freistehend · Kapelle | | Church · Chapel |
| Kloster · Klosterruine | | Monastery · Monastery ruin |
| Synagoge · Moschee | | Synagogue · Mosque |
| Schloss, Burg · Schloss-, Burgruine | | Palace, castle · Ruin |
| Turm · Funk-, Fernsehturm | | Tower · Radio-, TV-tower |
| Leuchtturm · Kraftwerk | | Lighthouse · Power station |
| Wasserfall · Schleuse | | Waterfall · Lock |
| Bauwerk · Marktplatz, Areal | | Important building · Market place, area |
| Ausgrabungs- u. Ruinenstätte · Bergwerk | | Arch. excavation, ruins · Mine |
| Dolmen · Menhir · Nuraghen | | Dolmen · Menhir · Nuraghe |
| Hünen-, Hügelgrab · Soldatenfriedhof | | Cairn · Military cemetery |
| Hotel, Gasthaus, Berghütte · Höhle | | Hotel, inn, refuge · Cave |

**Kultur**
Malerisches Ortsbild · Ortshöhe — **WIEN** (171) — **Culture** Picturesque town · Elevation

★★ **MILANO** — Eine Reise wert — Worth a journey

★ **TEMPLIN** — Lohnt einen Umweg — Worth a detour

**Andermatt** — Sehenswert — Worth seeing

**Landschaft**
Eine Reise wert — ★★ **Las Cañadas** — **Landscape** Worth a journey

★ **Texel** — Lohnt einen Umweg — Worth a detour

**Dikti** — Sehenswert — Worth seeing

**MARCO POLO Erlebnistour 1** — **MARCO POLO Discovery Tour 1**

**MARCO POLO Erlebnistouren** — **MARCO POLO Discovery Tours**

**MARCO POLO Highlight** — **MARCO POLO Highlight**

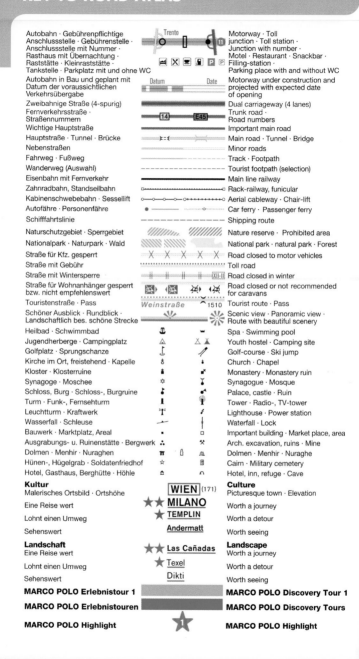

# FOR YOUR NEXT TRIP...

# MARCO POLO TRAVEL GUIDES

**A**lgarve
Amsterdam
Andalucia
Athens
Australia
Austria
**B**ali & Lombok
Bangkok
Barcelona
Berlin
Brazil
Bruges
Brussels
Budapest
Bulgaria
**C**alifornia
Cambodia
Canada East
Canada West / Rockies
& Vancouver
Cape Town &
Garden Route
Cape Verde
Channel Islands
Chicago & The Lakes
China
Cologne
Copenhagen
Corfu
Costa Blanca
& Valencia
Costa Brava
Costa del Sol & Granada
Crete
Cuba
Cyprus (North and
South)
**D**evon & Cornwall
Dresden
Dubai

Dublin
Dubrovnik &
Dalmatian Coast
**E**dinburgh
Egypt
Egypt Red Sea Resorts
**F**inland
Florence
Florida
French Atlantic Coast
French Riviera
(Nice, Cannes & Monaco)
Fuerteventura
**G**ran Canaria
Greece
**H**amburg
Hong Kong & Macau
**I**celand
India
India South
Ireland
Israel
Istanbul
Italy
**J**apan
Jordan
**K**os
Krakow
**L**ake Garda
Lanzarote
Las Vegas
Lisbon
London
Los Angeles
**M**adeira & Porto Santo
Madrid
Mallorca
Malta & Gozo
Mauritius
Menorca

Milan
Montenegro
Morocco
Munich
**N**aples & Amalfi Coast
New York
New Zealand
Norway
**O**slo
Oxford
**P**aris
Peru & Bolivia
Phuket
Portugal
Prague
**R**hodes
Rome
**S**alzburg
San Francisco
Santorini
Sardinia
Scotland
Seychelles
Shanghai
Sicily
Singapore
South Africa
Sri Lanka
Stockholm
Switzerland
**T**enerife
Thailand
Turkey
Turkey South Coast
Tuscany
**U**nited Arab Emirates
USA Southwest
(Las Vegas, Colorado,
New Mexico, Arizona
& Utah)
**V**enice
Vienna
Vietnam
**Z**akynthos & Ithaca,
Kefalonia, Lefkas

The travel guides with
Insider
Tips

# INDEX

This index lists all sights and destinations featured in this guide. Numbers in bold indicate a main entry.

Acharávi 30, **48**, 50, 52, 96, 103, 117
Achíllion **47**
Afiónas 22, **56**, 97, 114
Agía Ekateríni 52, **53**
Agías Efthímias, Kérkyra **34**, 102
Ágii Déka 119
Ágii Theodóri, Kérkyra 100
Ágios Géorgios Argirádon 16, 72, 98, 113
Ágios Géorgios North 16, 56, 97
Ágios Géorgios Pagón 16, 112, 113
Ágios Géorgios South **68**, 98
Ágios Górdis 16, 72, **73**, 98
Ágios Ioánnis **88**, 117, 122
Ágios Nikólaos Beach 83
Ágios Nikólas Gate, Kérkyra **38**
Ágios Spirídonas, Kérkyra **34**, 51, 53, 103
Ágios Stéfanos 16, **56,** 97, 132
Ágios Stéfanos Avlliotón 30, 78, 97
Ágios Stéfanos Siniés **61**, 104
Agní **61**
Almirós Beach 51
Alonáki 70
Análipsis 116
Anemómilos, Kérkyra 102
Angelókastro **66**, 67, 97
Áno Korakiána **84**, 102, 112
Aqualand 88, **117**
Archaeological Museum, Kérkyra **35**
Arillás **56**, 97, 113
Artemis Temple, Kérkyra 100

Astrakéri 53
Batería Beach 60
Benítses 77, 119, 122
British Cemetery, Kérkyra 36
Búkari **78**, 99
Butrint, Albania 108
Byzantine Museum, Kérkyra **36**, 40, 124
Cambiéllo, Kérkyra 37
Canal d'Amour 56
Cape Drástis 16, 48, **55**, 97
Cemetery church, Kérkyra 99
Chlómos 78
Corfu Trail 92, 112, 113
Dafníla **81**
Dassiá **81**, 84, 86, 95, 112, 115, 122
Doric Temple, Kérkyra 39, 101
Érmones 81, **92**, 111, 112
Esplanade, Kérkyra **37**, 40, 42, 115
Evstrámenou, Nímfes 53
Faliráki, Kérkyra 38
Folklore Museum, Sinarádes 93
Gardíki **72**, 98, 119
Gialiskári Beach 62
Glifáda 16, **88**, 90, 91
Guviá **86**, 95, **105**, 110, 112, 113
Hydropolis 52, **117**
Igoumenítsa 72
Ípsos 85
Kaizer's Throne **89**, 98
Kalámi **62**, 104
Kamináki Beach 62
Kanóni, Kérkyra **38**, 116
Kardáki Temple, Kérlyra 101
Kassiópi **58**, 104, 119
Káto Korakiána 84, 122
Kávos 17, **72**
Kérkyra 14, 17, **32**, 95, **99**, 102, 116, 118, 122,

123, 125, 126, 127
Komméno 83
Kontokáli **86**, 87, 112
Koríssion-See **69**, 98
Kulúra **62**, 104
Lákones 30, **67**, 97
Lefkími **72**, 98, 115
Makrádes 30, **67**, 97
Messongí **75**, 99, 118
Mirtiótissa 80, 81, **88**, 91
Mon Repos, Kérkyra **39**, 101
Moní Myrtidión 89
Moraítika 76
Néa Períthia 54
Néo Frúrio, Kérkyra 39
New Fort, Kérkyra 39
Nímfes **53**, 118
Nissáki 104
Nótos Beach 79, 99
Old Fort, Kérkyra 37, **40**, 119
Old Palace, Kérkyra 40
Pági 97
Paleó Períthia **54**, 103
Paleópolis Basilica, Kérkyra **40**, 100
Paleokastrítsa 16, **63**, 98, **106**, 111, 112, 119
Panagía Antivuniótissa, Kérkyra 36
Panagía Kassiópitra, Kassiópi 59
Panagía Mirtiótissa 89
Panagía Theotóku tis Paleokastrítsas 63
Pantokrátor 48, 54, 96, **102**
Paramónas **75**, 98
Páxos 111, 120
Pélekas 16, 80, 86, **88**, 98, 119
Pendáti **75**, 98
Perouládes 16
Peruládes 16, **55**, 97
Petríti 68, 72, **78**, 99
Pirgí 85
Pontikoníssi, Kérkyra **38**

# CREDITS

Róda **48**, 51, 96, 122
Ropa Valley **93**, 98, 112
Sidári **55**, 96
Sinarádes **93**, 98

Sokráki 29, **85**, 102
Strinílas 30, **56**, 102
Venetian shipyards,
Guviá 86

Vídos, Kérkyra 41
Vlachérna, Kérkyra **38**, 39

# WRITE TO US

e-mail: info@marcopologuides.co.uk

Did you have a great holiday?
Is there something on your mind?
Whatever it is, let us know!
Whether you want to praise, alert us
to errors or give us a personal tip –
MARCO POLO would be pleased to
hear from you.
We do everything we can to provide the
very latest information for your trip.

Nevertheless, despite all of our authors'
thorough research, errors can creep in.
MARCO POLO does not accept any
liability for this. Please contact us by
e-mail or post.

MARCO POLO Travel Publishing Ltd
Pinewood, Chineham Business Park
Crockford Lane, Chineham
Basingstoke, Hampshire RG24 8AL
United Kingdom

**PICTURE CREDITS**
Cover photograph: Cap Drástis (Schapowalow: R. Schmid)
Photographs: K. Bötig (68/69, 79, 85, 87, 120 bottom); Corbis: J. Andrew (7); Getty Images: L. Delderfield (9), A. Spatari (20/21), D. C. Tomlinson (8), van den Bergh (39, 121), A. M. Varela (18 bottom); Getty Images/Westend61 (3); R. Hackenberg (36, 67); huber-images: Dutton (28 left), R. Schmid (flap left, 4 bottom, 5, 14/15, 26/27, 47, 54/55, 59, 60, 107), G. Simeone (12/13, 62/63); F. Ihlow (31, 42); Laif: T. Linkel (29), T. & B. Morandi (32/33), Rodtmann (2), Trummer (64); Laif/hemis.fr: Gardel (11); E. Laue (50, 82); Look: Frei (30), H. Leue (41), H. Wohner (48/49); mauritius images: R. Eisele (119), M. Howard (6); mauritius images/age (108/109); mauritius images/ Alamy: J. Alamanou (118/119), Iconotec (73), kpzfoto (93), niftypics (28 right), A. Novelli (90); mauritius images/ blickwinkel: C. Ohde (19 bottom); mauritius images/Cultura (74); mauritius images/foodcollection (18 centre, 30/ 31, 120 top); mauritius images/imagebroker: K. Kreder (4 top, 57), N. Overy (97), N. Probst (10, 19 top, 34), Stella (53, 100/101); mauritius images/Prisma (94/95, 104/105); mauritius images/robertharding: T. Graham (22, 118); mauritius images/Westend61: C. Adams (18 top), E. Birk (25, 132/133), J. Fernow (117); Schapowalow: R. Schmid (1, 17); T. Stankiewicz (flap right, 45, 76, 80/81, 89); Transit-Archiv: Eisler (37); vario images/Westend61 (114/115); Visum: C. Oberste-Hedtbleck (110/111); Visum/MeystPhoto.com: F. Meyst (113); H. Wagner (70/71)

**3ʳᵈ Edition – fully revised and updated 2018**
Worldwide Distribution: Marco Polo Travel Publishing Ltd, Pinewood, Chineham Business Park,
Crockford Lane, Basingstoke, Hampshire RG24 8AL, United Kingdom. Email: sales@marcopolouk.com
© MAIRDUMONT GmbH & Co. KG, Ostfildern
Chief editor: Marion Zorn
Author: Klaus Bötig; Editor: Marlis von Hessert-Fraatz; Programme supervision: Lucas Forst-Gill, Susanne Heimburger, Nikolai Michaelis, Martin Silbermann, Kristin Wittemann
Picture editor: Gabriele Forst, Anja Schlatterer
What's hot: wunder media, Munich
Cartography road atlas: © MAIRDUMONT, Ostfildern; Cartography pull-out map: © MAIRDUMONT, Ostfildern
Design cover, p. 1, cover pull-out map: Karl Anders – Büro für Visual Stories, Hamburg; interior: milchhof:atelier, Berlin; design p. 2/3, Discovery Tours: Susan Chaaban Dipl.-Des. (FH)
Translated from German by Robert McInnes; Susan Jones; editor of the English edition: Christopher Wynne
Prepress: writehouse, Cologne; InterMedia, Ratingen
Phrase book in cooperation with Ernst Klett Sprachen GmbH, Stuttgart,
Editorial by Pons Wörterbücher

MIX
Paper from
responsible sources
FSC® C124385

# DOS & DON'TS 👆

A few things you should bear in mind on Corfu

## DON'T SHOW TOO MUCH SKIN

The Greeks have become used to naked skin in beach resorts. But further inland, many holidaymakers make fools of themselves by wearing too little. Your knees and shoulders must be covered in churches and monasteries.

## DON'T ACT LIKE THE PAPARAZZI

Many Corfiots like to be photographed if they are not exactly badly dressed or fear marriage problems. Before you release the shutter, smile at the person you want to photograph and wait for his or her agreement.

## DON'T UNDERESTIMATE THE DANGER OF FIRE

The risk of a forest fire on Corfu is high. Smokers should be especially careful.

## DON'T BE BROWBEATEN

Travel reps live from commissions. Most give honest information – but there are some black sheep who try to make their guests feel uncertain so that they will book their cars through them or take part in organised excursions instead of travelling by bus or taxi. Corfu is a safe island and there is no reason to be afraid of the locals.

## DON'T ASK ABOUT THE COMPETITION

Greeks are fairly honest. But, if you go into a taverna and ask about another one – you will be told that it doesn't exist, that the innkeeper has died or the police have closed it down.

## DON'T FORGET YOUR HIKING SHOES

Sandals are not even suitable for small hikes; you should at least wear sturdy trainers. The paths are often stony and slippery. And there are snakes – only a few and they are timid but you never know. Long trousers will protect you from thorns.

## DON'T LEAVE TARMACED ROADS

If you leave the main road in your hire car, you will be driving without insurance and will have to pay for any damage. On Corfu, damage to the underside and tyres of the car is never covered by insurance!

## DON'T BE SHOCKED BY THE PRICE OF FISH

Fresh fish has been extremely expensive in some Greek restaurants and tavernas for years. It is often sold by weight. You should ask how much a kilogram costs and be there when it is weighed so that you do not have any unpleasant surprises.